The Leadership Illusion

THE LEADERSHIP ILLUSION

ILLUSION

The Importance of Context
and Connections

Tony Hall

Karen Janman

palgrave
macmillan

First published 2010 by
PALGRAVE MACMILLAN

Palgrave Macmillan in the UK is an imprint of Macmillan Publishers Limited, registered in England, company number 785998, of Houndmills, Basingstoke, Hampshire RG21 6XS.

Palgrave Macmillan in the US is a division of St Martin's Press LLC, 175 Fifth Avenue, New York, NY 10010.

Palgrave Macmillan is the global academic imprint of the above companies and has companies and representatives throughout the world.

Palgrave® and Macmillan® are registered trademarks in the United States, the United Kingdom, Europe and other countries

ISBN 978-0-230-51656-4

This book is printed on paper suitable for recycling and made from fully managed and sustained forest sources. Logging, pulping and manufacturing processes are expected to conform to the environmental regulations of the country of origin.

A catalogue record for this book is available from the British Library.

A catalog record for this book is available from the Library of Congress.

10 9 8 7 6 5 4 3 2 1
19 18 17 16 15 14 13 12 11 10

Printed and bound in Great Britain by
CPI Antony Rowe, Chippenham and Eastbourne

Tony Hall

To
Mum and Dad: who would have guessed?
Tracey and Ethan: who always knew.

Karen Janman

To
My parents, Lawrie, Ollie and Maddy;
my past, my present and my future

CONTENTS

Acknowledgments   ix

Introduction: Making Connections and Shifting Perspectives   xi

1.   The Leadership Illusion   **1**
         Introduction   1
         The Mystique of Leadership   7
         From Attributes to Attributions   9
         Attributions and Castro's Gamble   10
         Through the Leadership Lens Obscurely: *Charisma*   13
         Conclusions   19

2.   Our Connected World   **22**
         Organizational Networks   26
         Personal Networks   34
         Parallel Lives   36
         The Case for Network Leadership   38

3.   The Right Sort of Social Capital   **40**
         Overview   40
         The Slippery Slopes of Social Capital   41
         Social Capital: A Brief Review   44
         The Problem with Putnam   48
         The Benefits of Social Capital   50
         Social Capital and its Implications For Leaders   57

4.   Making the Invisible Visible   **65**
         Introduction   65
         Social Network Analysis: Core Concepts   68

5.   Three Circles of Network Leadership   **85**
         Introduction   85
         The Future is Bright; the Future is Female?   86

Network Leadership: Connect and Deliver!   90
Network Leadership: A Deeper Dive   93
Final Thoughts: Squaring Circles And Praising Wine   109

6.   The Light Bulb Illusion   111
Innovation, Networks and Social Capital   116
Leadership and Innovation   123

7.   Leadership Development: Of Fires and Forges   127
Leadership Development and the Three Layers
of the Invisible   133
The Coaching Conundrum   145
From Fires to Forges   152

8.   Elephants, Moons and Mirrors   157
Mirrors in the Brain   163

Notes   166

Index   172

ACKNOWLEDGMENTS

This book has been a collaborative enterprise.

The contributions of many, many people have shaped the course and content; to them and all those friends and colleagues, who are as numerous as they are valued, we say "thank you."

However, there a few individuals that deserve a special mention. Our interviewees have profoundly contributed to the direction of our thinking and the arguments of the book as a whole. Amidst busy careers and hectic lives, they took time-out to answer the questions of two unpublished, unknown writers. Some of these accomplished people were already part of our world; others are new connections who brought fresh ideas and personal stories. Without their combined experience, insight and observations, this book would have remained too abstract, if indeed it would have been finished at all. To all those mentioned below, we owe you more than a small debt of gratitude and hope that the end result justifies the distraction from your commitments.

- Sir Christopher Evans, Chairman of Merlin Biosciences
- Peter Lidstone, European Supply Chain Director, Akzonobel Decorative Paints
- Andrew Kakabadse, Professor of International Management, Cranfield Management School
- Peter Scraton, Group HR Director, e2v
- Howard Bate, MD South Africa, Regional Director Africa, Mott MacDonald
- Eric Thomas, Vice Chancellor, Bristol University
- Kathy Sykes, Chair of Public Understanding of Science, Bristol University
- Clare Chapman, Director General of Workforce for NHS and Social Care, Department of Health, England
- Andrew Hargadon, Professor of Management, UC Davis Centre for Entrepreneurship
- Jez Cartright, CEO of Performance Consultants
- Stewart Milne, Chairman of Stewart Milne Group

- Ieda Gomes, VP New ventures, BP
- Will Hutton, Chairman of The Work Foundation
- Liz Bridge, Head of Learning Services, Cranfield School of Management
- Bruce Cronin, Greenwich Business School
- Ron Burt, Hobart W. Williams Professor of Sociology and Strategy, Chicago Booth School of Business

Aside from our interviewees, there are three people behind the scenes that we would like to thank explicitly:

- Stephen Rutt, our editor and a man who showed more than a little faith in the core idea
- Eleanor Davey Corrigan, our editorial assistant, for patience and good humor in the face of our ever-stretching deadlines
- Ollie Janman, Karen's son and our youngest critic, for his invaluable PowerPoint skills and insight when converting the paper scribbles of our various interviewees into the network maps that you see here.

Tony Hall and Karen Janman

INTRODUCTION

MAKING CONNECTIONS AND SHIFTING PERSPECTIVES

The 19th century was the century of the factory; whilst the 20th was the century of the office. The 21st century will be all about networks.
(Will Hutton, author of The State We're In*)*[1]

If there's something almost more interesting than the topic of leadership itself, it is the phenomenon of the endless, timeless torrent of writing *about* leadership. That constant stream has gushed into the world over thousands of years. From Sun Tzu to Cicero; from John Stuart Mill to Peter Drucker, the tide of opinion and perspectives shows no sign of receding. So we want to start this book by saying this will be the last book you will ever need to read on the topic of leadership. We want to, but we can't. It's not that our publisher has forbidden us from taking a monopolist's view of the market. And it isn't because we don't have faith in what we've written. We do. It's just impossible to nail down the secrets of leadership into a few smart remarks and a pocketful of behaviors. But over the years books about leadership have appeared in all shapes and guises, ranging from the accessible and experiential to the academic and the abstruse. They are likely to continue doing so for as long as we need leaders. In 470BC, in the Analects of Confucius, the author opined that leadership is, "To govern by virtue, let us compare it to the North Star: it stays in its place, while the myriad stars wait upon it."[2] At about the same time in the distant past, and interestingly also in China, Sun Tzu in *The Art of War* maintained that leadership is about "intelligence, trustworthiness, courage, sternness and humaneness."[3] No doubt the leadership debate, in one form or another, pre-dates these ancient texts, and it has certainly been a constant theme for writers, philosophers and leaders ever since.

In the twenty-first century, the topic remains, well, *topical*: a universally accepted definition still eluding the academics and the practitioners alike. The Editor of the business arm of this book's publisher receives a proposal for the next great thing in leadership every week. Every week! If you are a leader enthusiastically trying to tread the boards of self-development, or an HR professional desperately working on the next phase of leadership development for your "top team," where do you start? Try typing the word "leadership" into the Google search engine. How many results do you see? Millions: a bemusing result for anyone trying to understand what aspects of leadership, both in thinking and practice, might be relevant to contemporary life. What about adopting a more focused approach? Ignore Google; try Amazon. How many results do you get now? Has that helped? Probably not. Even within the constraints of a physical bookshop with a decent reputation, the leadership section is likely to leave you numb. So while we'd like to promise you that this is the last thing you will ever need to read about leadership, the bulky weight of history tells us this is unlikely to be the case. What we can promise you is an important argument about why the essence of leadership has been so hard to grasp.

***

The BFI Imax cinema near Waterloo in central London is a wonder. Its gargantuan, wrap-around screen and the immersive acoustic capability has terrified and delighted our children over the last few years. However, today (without the children) the object of our attention is cellular not celluloid. We've come to listen to a presentation from Malcolm Gladwell, author of *The Tipping Point*[4] and *Blink*.[5] He's over here from the United States to talk to us about his latest book: *Outliers: The Story of Success*.[6] Aside from being fans, we're here because while the dust jacket will tell you this book is all about "achievement," it's also about leadership.

We sit down into the plushly upholstered seats; they are dangerously comfortable for these mid-week, mid-morning seminars. There is quite a crowd today for the session, certainly more than we've seen at recent events at the same venue. The Man Himself is lounging against the barrier in front of the first row, patiently waiting for our gaggle to settle down. Malcolm Gladwell is a curious looking individual. He's slight with spindly fingers and a mop of hair that defies gravity in an Einstein sort of way. He has a gaze that seems to take everything in, and, one imagines, a brain that constantly organizes the world around him into a continuous stream of compelling stories. When he begins his talk, there is no PowerPoint. He tells his story with cannily chosen words, carried by a gentle voice that needs the help of the microphone and the sound system. This is not your typically brazen proclamation from your typical business guru.

Although not all the "Story of Success" is outlined during Gladwell's session, the essence of the book is that great achievement for anyone in any field can be attributed to three factors: talent, a huge amount of practice (10,000 hours of practice to be precise) and opportunity. In short, it's about the interplay between the individual and the environment, and that's what determines success, not the individual alone.

At the beginning of "Outliers," Gladwell tells the tale of Italian farm workers who emigrated to the United States during the later nineteenth century, building a community in Bangor, Pennsylvania. In many ways, these Italians were no different from waves of other emigrants who arrived in America during this period; they were hardworking, optimistic and flocked together in settlements where they re-established some of the ways of the "Old Country." However, there was something remarkable about these specific settlers: the men had an incredibly low incidence of heart disease. Doctors came to study these healthy men who originated from the Italian province of Foggia. They studied their physiology, but found nothing remarkable there. They scrutinized their dietary traditions, assuming that they had imported a balanced approach to nutrition, but again, they found nothing of note. Eventually, after observing not the individuals but the community, the answer was found. The secret to their low incidence of heart problems was their social traditions; the way in which many generations of family lived together, the way in which people supported each other. This had stumped the doctors and the researchers because, as Gladwell points out: "They had to look beyond the individual. They had to understand the culture he or she was part of . . . They had to appreciate the idea that the values of the world we inhabit and the people we surround ourselves with have a profound effect on who we are." Our rationale for spilling yet more ink onto the leadership page stems from that same, simple argument. Leadership is about the individual **and** the social context and connections that he or she creates and inhabits.

By early 2009, the tightly wound global economy had unraveled at an unprecedented pace. The Confederation of British Industry (CBI), the voice of British Industry, published their view of the state of the nation. In their eyes, the most shocking aspect of the situation was not necessarily the lack of liquidity in the markets, the falling house prices, a rising needle of unemployment or the incredible difficulties faced by high street traders over the 2008 Christmas season; no, the most shocking aspect was the speed at which the economy had imploded. When up against that sheer pace of change, then the symbiotic relationship between leader and their social context becomes even more important because without the right sort of relationships, a leader is just another Sisyphus, all alone and pushing a very heavy stone up an extremely steep hill. Those relationships and those connections enable the right sort of leader – more of which later – to make the most of two very important processes: anticipation and adaptation. Adaptation enables the leader, and by extension his or her organization to learn from collective experience; while anticipation helps to ride the next wave or opportunity or calamity.

Aside from its rapidity, twenty-first century change can be complex and multifaceted. Nevertheless, we see a convergence of contextual factors that have important consequences for leaders and their leadership approach. Here are a few of those recurring features that we see in everyday organizational life:

1. The blurring of boundaries and increasing interdependence within or between individuals, organizations and countries. We are tied, yoked and snared together financially, technologically and culturally in ways that would have been unimaginable fifty years ago;
2. A shift in emphasis from a complete reliance on formal structures and contractual transactions to a greater dependence on informal relationships and agreements;
3. The growing importance of technology to develop and sustain connections between people for a variety of purposes, for example, the myriad of Internet-based business models that increasingly consume a larger market share across a variety of sectors; social networking sites such as Facebook, Skype for business and personal conversations; Twitter for micro-blogging.

The web of connections – the networks – that emerge from these different modes of human interaction invite leaders to adopt a different approach to lead successfully with the emergent complexity, the uncertainty and the interdependence inherent within our heavily latticed world.

It has to be said that although we believed that everything you've just read constituted an argument for *thinking* differently about leadership, we weren't convinced that we should be *writing* about leadership. We were still of the mind that too many trees, too much shelf space and excessive "self space" had been dedicated to the name of leadership. It wasn't until we started to discuss those ideas with real people, in a variety of settings and organizations that we began to believe there may be some practical purpose in the broader approach to leadership described in this book.

The flow of those discussions; some private and some public, with academics and development practitioners, and some with leaders and their followers, led to four conversational "eddies." These recurring themes finally led to us to putting thumb and finger to keyboard. They are sketched out below:

1. **Context is king:** most people writing about leadership, either recently or in times gone by, have tended to focus exclusively on the individual. Almost without exception, writers have ignored the importance of the broader social and organizational context. We shouldn't be surprised. The reductionist approach of modern science, an approach that strives for problems and their solutions to be neatly segmented into discrete, individual parts, would always have its influence on our views of leadership. It's an approach that leads to "tick box" leadership development, where aspiring leaders give up on the possibility of their own leadership potential when confronted with an impossibly aspirational list of personal qualities.

2. **Time changes everything:** another facet of the contemporary leadership cannon is the need to establish leadership attributes that are discrete and immutable. Our own viewpoint is that effective leadership is adaptive. It doesn't remain the same, irrespective of the context. Are we really to believe that the leadership of an eighteenth-century factory in Great Britain is the same as the sort of leadership that brings success to a modern day social enterprise? Leaders in this sense are agents of change whose success or failure will be in part determined by their qualities and talents, partly by the pattern of opportunity and adversity in the surrounding environment at any point in time. We will argue that while there may be some general principles of leadership, the relative importance of those principles and the underpinning behaviors will change over time as the environment changes.

3. **Joining the dots**: Our third premise is that too much thinking and writing about leadership comes from a single "thought silo." Rather than drawing on a range of disciplines, authors are too inclined to fit their thoughts about leadership into a specific and familiar discipline. Leadership is not the only field of inquiry to suffer this myopia, but there is a trend in other fields that interdisciplinary investigation is becoming more prevalent and yields insights that otherwise would not have been possible. In this book, we have plundered ideas from whatever sources we have seen as relevant in order to develop our own argument.

4. **Network leadership**: finally, we regard the concept of networks, and the practice of network mapping, as critical to understanding the social, economic and organizational context of the present and the immediate future. Furthermore, understanding personal networks will be central to the success of leaders in organizations regardless of whether they are in the private, public or the voluntary sectors.

Your reading journey of the next 180 pages or so will take you through the following "mind stones":

- A critique of leadership, and writing about leadership, that explores why so much popular thinking is fallacious and illusory
- An introduction to networks that highlights their prevalence in a multitude of forms and which support a plethora of purpose
- An outline of the common principles and dynamic behaviors that help people achieve their goals through their networks (network leadership), particularly in organizations that have moved to flatter, less hierarchical structures and which are committed to building motivation in the pursuit of high performance
- A run-through of the general characteristics of social networks and the process of mapping those networks. We'll outline some of the pitfalls associated with these techniques, but also how to make the most out of understanding the pattern of relationships that emerge from the results.
- We'll specifically cover the importance of networks, innovation and leadership. We'll explore the myth of the lone inventor and what sorts of networks are most likely to result in greater creativity and more innovation.

- Finally, we'll think about how best to develop leadership skills, offering a critique of certain current practices and approaches such as coaches and workshops.

As we write these words, we are wondering whether or not we will make some sort of connection – emotional, intellectual and meaningful – with you, the reader. This may sound like a sloppy, sentimental opening to a second-rate, self-help book, but it is nevertheless an honest expression of our joint intent. If our words don't have resonance and relevance, there is really no point in adding to the mountain of literature in this field. We want this book to create a degree of engagement with the idea of leadership that surmounts the constraints of the printed word. Why? Because this book is all about the importance of connections – networks or "webs" of connections – and the growing and inevitable importance of these webs for organizations of all sizes, shapes and purpose. These particular paragraphs are being written in a small cottage perched on the edge of a cliff during winter in Cornwall. Ironically, to capture these words on digital paper, we have tried to slip the gravitational pull of our own networks – professional, personal and technological – and have arrived at a remote though beautiful destination where the displays on our mobile phones formally announce "No network coverage." The isolation, however, is an illusion. The research and preparation for writing this book has been a process of connecting with people, their work and the challenges of their leadership roles. These connections remain in place despite the temporary failure of technology. Our role now is to connect you, the unknown reader, through the words on the page, with the web of experience that has shaped and informed the content of this book.

Finally, an important principle we have adhered to in researching this book is to avoid at all costs a purely theoretical dissertation. So we have peppered the content of this book with first-person case histories of leaders from a range of organizations. They are drawn from a range of backgrounds and professions: entrepreneurs, business people across a variety of sectors, vice-chancellors of sprawling universities, media experts and politicians. These leaders are faced with the daily challenges of "network leadership," in both the public and the private sectors; we have explored with these people how they think, feel and behave, in meeting those challenges. We have identified the common themes from their individual stories but have tried, wherever possible, to allow the individual to describe their experiences in their own words in order to retain a sense of immediacy and impact.

The book itself is an eclectic web of ideas, research, thinking and, perhaps most importantly, experience. In particular, it is based on the experience of leaders who find themselves embedded in complex networks of people, processes, stakeholders, commercial opportunities and competitors, and who are, or have been, challenged to nurture, develop and, at the right moment, destroy existing networks in order to achieve diverse organizational and personal goals. Our arguments cover a range of disciplines including cognitive psychology, social psychology, sociology, network science, complexity science, organizational behavior and economics. The style of the book is fundamentally interdisciplinary because it is the authors' belief that in the search for answers to significant questions in the twenty-first century, horizontal synergies are essential for developing coherent and cogent responses. In short, the content of the book does try to walk its own talk.

A final thought: If the style and diverse content of this book hit their mark, we should achieve the author-reader connections that we are hoping for. If not, you can frequently find us in pubs across London, railing against the latest fad in the leadership cannon, and sinking the odd pint of beer.

1

THE LEADERSHIP ILLUSION

INTRODUCTION

Illusions are either natural or man-made. When a full moon hovers low in the night sky, luminous and seemingly much larger than usual, our eyes are deceived by its proximity to the horizon. Our perceptual system makes a faulty calculation about the moon's actual size but it's a perfectly natural mistake. The two rings in Figure 1.1 create an illusion of two rings interlocking. Look more closely and it becomes apparent that the circles and their *perceived* connectivity are actually impossible figures. This is an artist's illusion, an intentional sleight of mind that takes advantage of the way evolution has shaped the way we perceive and interpret depth, shape and three-dimensional space. The key difference between these two illusions is that if we concentrate

FIGURE 1.1 **Interlocking rings**

hard on the latter we can begin to see through the deception; try as we might with the moon illusion, our perceptual error continues. No matter how long we stare at the moon, even when we know the science we can never persuade our perceptual system to construct in our mind's eye a more accurately sized view of this lunar landscape. This book is about what we have called the "leadership illusion": a naturally occurring, inevitably biased and fundamentally flawed view of leaders and their worlds. The leadership illusion is not a new phenomenon – it has been fooling us since our conscious minds began to grapple with the nature of leadership. And neither is it an atypical aspect of human perception. The field of psychology abounds with examples where our "commonsense" view of the everyday world is deceived by the way in which our brains reconstruct the raw, confusing data that bombard our sensory systems every second into a world we recognize and understand. However, the leadership illusion is the start and not the end point of this book. This is just our springboard to argue the importance of context and connections when thinking about leaders and leadership. Before we explore the broad implications of this perceptual effect for how we understand leaders, the nature of leadership and our own leadership potential, we need to spend some time understanding it better. And to really understand the underlying nature of the leadership illusion, which helps to develop a fresh and more reliable perspective on leadership – one that may be useful for the present and the future – it's helpful to go back to the past.

The year 1915 was important for understanding illusions. In the middle of the mindless slaughter that was World War I, Albert Einstein had a breakthrough. Finally, he had the equations necessary for him to publish with confidence his paper on the General Theory of Relativity. His paper changed the way we see, not just our world, but the universe itself. Einstein's ideas turned our existing understanding of the laws of physics upside-down and demonstrated how our intuitive perception of the world around us can be easily duped. For many years, those who thought themselves to be "in-the-know" had seen the universe through Newtonian spectacles: a world of discrete and separate bodies, orbiting each other, but never connecting. Einstein's genius was to escape the gravitational pull of those concepts and to propose a radically different perspective. When pushed to capture this new thinking in a single sentence, Einstein replied, "Time and space and gravitation have no separate existence from matter." A crazy idea to many at the time; and difficult to understand even today. Nevertheless Einstein had seen through the illusion of discontinuity and enabled us to see a more connected universe than we had previously perceived.

Two hundred and twenty three miles away, insulated from World War I by a declaration of neutrality, Denmark stood back from the hostilities of 1915. Although not a culture where people are encouraged to stand out from the crowd, Denmark has a rich and striking intellectual heritage with a rich vein of names of those that are instantly recognizable. Søren Kirkegaard, Hans Christian Andersen and Niels Bohr are all Danes who have distinguished themselves not only in Danish society but also across the international community. In 1915, Edgar Rubin, a Danish psychologist, was part of this Danish tradition of leading thinkers. Working in Copenhagen, Rubin was committed to understanding the mechanisms of perception. He developed several illusions to highlight how something we take so much for granted – i.e. how we see the world about us – is a complex psychological phenomenon.

Take a look at Figure 1.2. This is one of several classic optical illusions originally developed by Edgar Rubin. The image can be perceived as either an outline of a vase *or* two faces in profile. Depending on who

FIGURE 1.2 **Rubin's vase**

(*Source:* http://en.wikipedia.org/wiki/index.html?curid=8254483 Free access)
Credit John Smithson 2007

3

we are and our experience, we will either see the vase or the faces first; then alternate our perception between the two. We never see both images simultaneously. Even though we *know* that the figure contains two images, the limits of our perceptual system allow us to focus our attention on only one recognizable image at a time.

> When two fields have a common border, and one is seen as figure and the other as ground, the immediate perceptual experience is characterized by a shaping effect which emerges from the common border of the fields and which operates ... **more strongly on one than on the other**.
>
> (Edgar Rubin, Synsoplevede Figurer, 1915)[1]

Rubin's vase illustrates exactly what we have in mind when we talk about the "leadership illusion": it is the hardwired habit of writers, researchers and leaders themselves, when examining the causes of success or failure, to focus predominantly on the individual (sometimes the context), but very rarely both *at the same time*. We want our answers to such fundamentally important questions to be elegantly expedient. Why? A complex, conscious analysis of the infinite number of informational variables given in any context, confounded by an attempt at really understanding how they interact with the rich diversity of human nature, is not a route to quick decision making. And as someone once said, "there's the quick and the dead." Our minds incline toward the instant and the seemingly obvious because instinctively we assume this is more likely to help our own survival. Order is better than deep complexity, regardless of information lost. In the case of Rubin's vase, our perceptual system organizes the data contained in the image so that we can make sense of what we see. And see it quickly. To see someone as either fabulously successful or woefully inadequate is to be seduced by an evolutionary need for predictive control over our environment. We like our solutions in neat boxes to satisfy this need. And the way we perceive our leaders is no exception.

Consider Jeff Skilling, ex-CEO of the now-defunct energy company Enron. What sort of leader was he? To the business cognoscenti during the late nineties, a time when Enron enjoyed profits aplenty, Skilling was something to behold – a prince of a big corporate enterprise to whom the great and the good were happy to pay homage. This was Jeff's time. All the world was his stage, and everyone loved the Skilling show. At the time, he was seen as a risk-loving, charismatic leader who would "think nothing of racing a motor bike 1,000 miles across Mexico." Twenty years before, Skilling had streaked out of Harvard Business School in the top five percent of his year, scorched a red-hot reputation in McKinsey and, almost inevitably, was adopted by Ken Lay, then CEO of Enron in 1991. During the rest of this most decadent of decades, Jeff forged his name as *the* entrepreneur for big business. Skilling cannily recognized that the inherent volatility of the gas sales market offered opportunity galore for Enron. Plying the principle of "knowledge is power" to the full, Skilling used Enron's intimate understanding of those market conditions, derived from being the owner of the largest gas pipeline in the US, to become an online energy trading company. Enron then moved to offer major customers long-term fixed contracts for gas, clearly attractive to the clients because it brought potential stability to the usually volatile cost associated with an organization's energy utilization. Skilling and his crew then applied their market knowledge to minimize their own risk through the use of financial derivatives – those complex, arcane financial tools that lay at the heart of Baring's collapse. Ken Lay, clearly enamored by Skilling's apparent brilliance, declared that Jeff "didn't have a non-strategic bone in his body." This was in an article confidently identifying the top 50 CEO's for 1999, 2000 and 2001.

This was all before The Fall. At the beginning of 2001, Enron was still regarded by Fortune Magazine as being one of the Top 100 companies to work for; by November 30, 2001, Enron had declared itself bankrupt. Some five years later, at the end of a trial that had taken four years and the jury a further four months to reach a decision, Jeff Skilling was found guilty on nineteen charges of corporate malfeasance, concluding one of the most serious cases of business fraud of recent times. From charismatic and confident to arrogant and avaricious, the changing story of Jeffrey Skilling has been played out in blogs and biographies across the world ever since. Chuck Salter, a writer for the business magazine *Fast Company*, on the day of the jury's decision, blogged smugly about how an early interview with Skilling on the topic of leadership had not been published because it was full of "platitudes and self-promotion." In the eyes of the world, Skilling had shifted from a neat box labeled "hero" to a boldly branded "zero." And while some writers have made a half-hearted stab at placing his actions within a broader context, not least of which was his former boss Tom Peters, the between-the-lines conclusion is that Jeff Skilling must have been lacking some fundamental moral fiber. It's his conscience, not his context, which had been found lacking.

What was Jeff Skilling – charismatic leader or moral bankrupt? Or both? Or neither? Did a culture of corruption at Enron in someway tacitly encourage his actions? And what about the wider context – the nineties themselves? David Remnick, staff writer with the *New Yorker*, called the nineties a "New Gilded Age – a moment of prosperity, satisfaction and self-satisfaction … rife with contradictions."[2] It must have been a challenging time to lead any organization into unchartered economic waters. Were the 1990s, as declared in *USA Today*, "an era of unparalleled human greed"? And if they were, how did the moral undertow drag this once Harvard hotshot into believing he could mystify the market and fool the federal government?

In 2009, Malcolm Gladwell, staff writer for the *New Yorker* and author of *The Tipping Point* described Skilling as the "canary in the cage" for the financial markets.[3] He was referring to the practice by miners in the early part of the twentieth century to take a canary down into the mines to check for poisonous gas. The sensitive respiratory system of the canary acted as an early warning device. If the subterranean atmosphere became noxious: the canary invariably responded to the poison by falling off its perch early enough for the miners to make a life-saving retreat.

When Skilling fell off his lofty perch, perhaps the world should have taken more account of the context and less of the man. Although Skilling and his men bullied, cajoled, cheated and charmed their way to ruin, the nature of the precipitous collapse of the financial markets from mid-2007 to late 2008 suggests they were not alone. Bill Lerach was the attorney, who acted on behalf of the Enron shareholders. In the documentary "Smartest Guys in the Room," which dramatically unravels the Enron collapse, Lerach had this to say about the web of deception in which Skilling operated:

> The Enron fraud is the story of synergistic corruption. There are supposed to be checks and balances. The lawyers are supposed to say no, the accountants are supposed to say no, the bankers are supposed to say no. No one who was supposed to say no, said no. They all took their share of the money from the fraud and put it in their pocket.[4]

The context and connections around Skilling created a world where anything seemed possible for him and his traders to make money, and where he was truly a Master of his perceived Universe. Where does the influence and effect of the environment end and the leader begin? Does Skilling fit into a simple box labeled "hero" or "zero"? Our argument is that to make sense of leadership, we have to make sense of the context as well – because both are inextricably interlinked. The constant argument in this book, at times implicit – but always present, is that to elude the leadership illusion we have to ignore our innate preference for what, intuitively, seems "obvious." As human beings, our judgment is frequently flawed and perhaps none more so than when we consider our leaders with admiring or damning eyes.

THE MYSTIQUE OF LEADERSHIP

Jeff Skilling is not an isolated example. Most of us have been seduced at some time by the leadership illusion and, often, those who should have a clearer view only succeed in obfuscating the topic further. Leadership – both theory and practice – is characterized by complexity, contradiction and confusion. Every leader, and every writer about leadership, has his or her own particular view about the "essence" of great leadership. Successful CEOs, such as Bill Gates, freely express their views about the subject based on their own experiences, but the results of these idiosyncratic and subjective analyses are seldom consistent. But professional researchers and leadership observers fare no better.

Richard Chait (2004), Professor of Leadership at Harvard Graduate School of Education, recently presented an audience with the many paradoxes that can be found in the leadership literature. He compared researchers in this area to "organizational meteorologists"; his view being that we have as much chance of predicting whether it will rain or shine three weeks hence as we have of reliably finding ourselves a suitable leader. Not an entirely encouraging analogy for anyone interested in the leadership trade. This situation is not helped by established voices in the field wrapping the subject in an aura of mystique. Consider this quote from Warren Bennis, a leading thinker in the leadership field for many years:

> To an extent, leadership is like beauty; it's hard to define, but you know it once you've seen it.

This quote is taken from Warren Bennis' book *On Becoming a Leader*, an engaging and thoughtful view of the leadership domain, summarizing over forty years of thinking and writing on the subject.[5] In this one, pithy phrase, Bennis, the "grandfather guru" of the leadership field, is addressing the central issue for those of us trying to understand leadership more clearly: *what is it?* His argument here is that leadership is not amenable to a definition of scientific precision, but that nevertheless we are all able to recognize a great leader when we see one.

Essentially, this amounts to Bennis capitulating grandly when it comes to pinning down what leadership is really about. And he's not alone. Rudolf Giuliani, Mayor of New York from 1994 to 2001, won international acclaim for great and tenacious leadership after supporting New York through the aftermath of 9/11. In Giuliani's high profile book *Leadership*, published in 2004, he reinforces this sort of approach: "the truth is that a big part of leadership is mysterious. Inspiration must be taken wherever and whenever it comes."[6] Even in the midst of this purportedly practical guide to leadership, Giuliani cannot help but introduce an ineffable quality to the topic.

In one sense it should come as no surprise that leadership is a slippery notion: there is a glorious array of philosophies and perspectives, languages and vocabulary on offer when elucidating any form of human behavior. We may have a practitioner or an academic approach; we may adopt a positivist or post-modern viewpoint; we may offer a metaphorical or psychological perspective; we may even hitch our leadership wagon to the power of pure allegory. And we may embrace all of these possible viewpoints within the course of a single paragraph. In short, our reference point is not always the same and it can be bloody confusing. And those of us who have an interest in leadership are not alone. Novelists, artists, poets and playwrights have struggled to vividly articulate the meaning of what it is to be human for thousands of years. Why should our attempts to elucidate and illustrate great leadership be any easier – isn't that part of the subject's attraction?

So what is the best we can hope for – to find our leaders through a combination of serendipity and second sight? Is our perceptual apparatus to be continuously enthralled by the leadership illusion? Perhaps a better understanding of the psychological mechanisms underpinning those perceptions will steer us in the right direction, in particular, recognizing the important distinction between the notion of an "attribute" and the psychological process of "attribution."

FROM ATTRIBUTES TO ATTRIBUTIONS

To a greater or lesser extent, we are all psychologists. The popularity of reality TV shows, from *Big Brother* to *Survivor*, may stem (at least partially) from our need to explain and predict someone else's behavior. There is no doubt some evolutionary advantage is afforded by the ability to "mind read": neuroscientists now have more than enough evidence to argue the existence of areas in our brain dedicated to understanding the crafty intentions of others. There seems to be commercial advantage, too. In a 2006 edition of *American Scientific Mind*,[7] journalists reported on how "empathy training" has added to the bottom line of many organizations. The evidence that training people actually helps us to understand how someone else is thinking suggests that empathy is no mean feat. And empathy itself can't be useful unless there are consistent aspects of personality that ultimately help us to predict behavior. It is the existence of empathy itself that contributes to our belief that to understand the person is to understand the leader. The assumption is itself fundamental to an attribute-based approach to leadership. How do we go about understanding that unique constellation of idiosyncratic but enduring attributes which in sum we call 'personality'?

The word "personality" is derived from the Latin word "persona," meaning mask. In Latin, the sense of the word mask is different from how we use it today. In common parlance a mask is something that hides someone's personality. In Latin the term refers to the essence of someone's character. It is the latter interpretation that broadly describes the meaning of "personality": a range of attributes, (which may involve thoughts, feelings and behaviors) that endures over time and which gives form and shape to who we are as individuals. Psychology has approached this science of personality in a number of different ways, giving birth to a range of subdisciplines, all of which aspire to be the Rosetta stone of human nature.

Similarly, in the leadership literature, there has been an ocean of taxonomies that has tried to capture the enduring attributes of leaders. They have been drawn on psychological models past and present, ranging from psychoanalytic to cognitive to behavioral perspectives. All have in common the assumption that the success of a leader can be pinned down to enduring and intrinsic aspects of the individual character.

Attribute-based approaches are as many as they are diverse. Two of the more engaging and recent examples include Howard Gardner's cognitive theory of leadership[8] and, from the UK, Beverley Alimo-Metcalfe's explicitly behavioral take on transformational leadership.[9] Gardner, described by the *New York Times* as "one of the most interesting American psychologists" published his thoughts in a book titled *Leading Minds: An Anatomy of Leadership*. Gardner argued that a key attribute of great leaders was the ability to tell stories that captured the hearts and minds of their followers, and offered a cognitive framework, that is, purely psychological, to explain how they achieved this. While the details of his theory are not explored here (although well worth reading), Gardner's approach is typical of an attribute-centered view of leadership. In complete contrast is Alimo-Metcalfe's view that leadership can be summed up in a number of behavioral clusters called leadership "competencies." For her, leadership is not about how you think; it's about how you behave. Based on her exhaustively empirical model, leadership itself can be captured in nine or ten of these competencies. Both of these researchers come to the leadership problem from diametrically opposed perspectives, but they share the single assumption that understanding leadership is about understanding attributes.

A curious example of the attribute-based approach can be seen in Rubenzer and Faschingbauer's trait-based evaluation of American presidents.[10] They analyzed American presidents through the lens of a psychological profiling tool that deconstructs personality into five independent traits. In their fascinating book *Personality, Character and Leadership in the White House*, they clustered presidential leadership styles according to common traits, as evaluated through the eyes of biographers, historians and close advisors. For example, they group together Roosevelt, Delano and Kennedy as "extraverts" and Jackson, Johnson and Nixon as "Dominators." Although on the surface this appears to be a consideration of presidential and leadership attributes, in truth it is more about attribution. They are in fact making inferences about leadership based on the perceptions of other people. Time to consider what this means in more detail.

ATTRIBUTIONS AND CASTRO'S GAMBLE

Attributions are the inferences we make about people that typically go beyond the available information. If someone cuts in front of us while driving on the motorway, forcing us to break hard as a consequence, we are quick to make a judgment about the driver's skills and personality.

His context – perhaps a member of his family that has taken seriously ill – is unknown to us, so we base our conclusions about character on the behavior that we see. However, psychologists have shown us that time after time, even when there is a glut of contextual information freely available, our faulty perceptual mechanisms over-emphasize character and underplay context. In the psychology trade, they call this the "Fundamental Attribution Error" (FAE) and it lies at the heart of the leadership illusion.

> Condemn me, it does not matter; history will absolve me.
>
> (Fidel Castro, 1953)[11]

Fidel Castro has taken a gamble on his own immortality: he has speculated that history will judge him more favorably than his contemporaries. A man of contradiction, Castro is the revolutionary who became one of the longest-serving prime ministers the world has seen, a seamless shift from anarchist to social architect of a new Establishment. His leadership style has been described anywhere from the dictatorial to inspirational, and everything in-between: a reputation forged in the political heat of Cuban life. Castro's approach to dealing with his opponents has been harsh and uncompromising, but he resolutely believes that historical analysts at some point in the future will loudly congratulate his contribution and his vision. In other words, Castro is hoping that future generations will place his actions into a wider context, and finally recognize that perhaps the ends justified the means. It is an expectation founded on the assumption that human beings are able to evaluate their leaders through the complex mixture of circumstance and personality. It is ironic, then, that a famously *failed* experiment by Edward E. Jones, an experiment that had been designed to demonstrate irrefutably that human beings *do* take contextual factors into account when making decisions about people, used pro-Castro speeches as a critical experimental element.

In 1967, five years after the Cuban Missile Crisis had brought the planet to the brink, Jones and Harris conducted an experiment which they believed would demonstrate how human beings utilize situational information when drawing inferences about people.[12] They randomly assigned the people participating in the study into two groups prior to listening to essays. Political science students who had adopted an unequivocally positive view about Castro had written the essays. Everyone was asked to listen to the speech and subsequently rate how pro-Castro they believed the author to be. Half of these people were told that the authors of the essays had *chosen* to write on this topic; the other half of the group was told that the authors had been randomly assigned the topic based on the flip of the coin. Not unreasonably, Jones and Harris predicted that in the "randomly assigned" category, people would assign a lower pro-Castro rating than the other group – after all, these people had not chosen to write a positive essay on this man. They were wrong – the results showed no real difference between the ratings of the two groups; both groups rated the authors as being equally pro-Castro. All contextual information had been ignored when making inferences about the political preferences of the authors.

Although it never became the "Fundamental Attribution Error" until named, some say provocatively, by Lee Ross in 1977,[13] this pervasive psychological effect has become one of the most researched perpetual biases in social psychology. While some might argue that it is a "robust and ubiquitous finding," understanding it has been trickier than some imagined. Explanations as to why this occurs fall into two separate, but probably related, schools of thought. The first argument maintains that the FAE is essentially a cognitive shortcut that enables us to make sense of the mass of data that impinges on our sensory systems. This is a line of thinking not dissimilar to the effect associated with Rubin's vase at the beginning of the chapter. The second argument is that this is a by-product of our goal-oriented behavior – it helps us to predict and control the world about us. Although some psychologists have argued that these explanations are mutually exclusive, it is also reasonable to argue they are part and parcel of the same effect: if we are to quickly and efficiently predict what is happening in the world around us, we have to pick on the most salient information in front of us and use that to draw our conclusions. Perhaps evolutionary experience has helped us understand that, when it comes to gambling on personal survival, ignoring the myriad of situational cues and broad contextual information and placing greater emphasis on personal attributes is an effective method for improving our odds. This coarse form of intuitive analysis may have been helpful when considering human motivation generally, but when it comes to a systematic understanding of leadership, the process is found wanting. Consider Jeff Skilling: drawing inferences about his leadership and ignoring the wider context can lead to some rash assumptions.

But psychology is as full of contradictions as the human beings it sets out to explain. There is evidence to indicate that the FAE is a pattern of thinking that is learned through experience, as we get older. Some psychologists have found that young children are free from this cognitive bias; only in late childhood do they begin to fall foul of dispositional attributions. To complicate matters more, in certain quarters, there is the belief that the FAE is not something that is apparent across all cultures. The cultural shift occurs, or so some argue, when we compare the effect in individualist, or Western, cultures, to what happens in collectivist, or Eastern, cultures. The jury appears to be out on this particular debate: more recent evidence indicates that in China, India and Taiwan, the FAE does manifest itself. Perhaps we should not be surprised by this. In the flattened world described by Thomas Friedman in his recent book *The World is Flat*,[14] the increasing connectedness of the world will be accompanied by a process of cultural homogenization. Whether Friedman is correct about the eventual "rounding" of cultural differences, the FAE is a pervasive aspect of our psyche that is not going away.

In summary, attributes and attributions are both important factors when we come to try to understand human nature generally and leadership specifically. Both approaches have something useful to tell us. There are some aspects, some attributes, of an individual that make them successful as a leader. But we need to evaluate the person and the context in order to be clearer about whether what we perceive is real or illusory. The pervasive effect of the FAE lies at the heart of the leadership illusion, and should not be discounted whenever we are considering the qualities that leaders bring to any situation. And we'd do well to remember that the FAE is an inevitable consequence of our mind's inclination toward the simple and the straightforward. To make this point more practically, let's have a look at one of the great imponderables in the leadership literature: charisma.

THROUGH THE LEADERSHIP LENS OBSCURELY: *CHARISMA*

Charisma is a word that has forever bedeviled and bedazzled our view of leadership. It's been used in an explanatory sense to describe the success of leaders all over the world, and in many different contexts. Western studies of leadership are littered with eulogizing exemplars of charismatic leaders: John F. Kennedy, Winston Churchill, Steve Jobs and Richard Branson. In 2006, Jobs seems to have cornered the market for being regarded as a charismatic business leader. A recent biography by Young and Simon, *iCon*,[15] began their genuinely critical review of his career by arguing that he had been "bestowed with the gift" of charisma, and presented him as an "evangelist of the digital age." However, we shouldn't think that charisma is by any means an exclusively Western phenomenon.

Take the leadership of Singapore. This Asian city-state has established itself as a hub of Asian economic activity. Described by the *Economist* as being "one of Asia's – and the world's – most important financial centers," the World Economic Forum declared in 2005 that it is "the world's most competitive economy in information technology." Not a bad accolade for a country of only 4.2 million citizens (as a reference point, London has approximately 7.3 million). A city of contradictions and contrasts, the dazzling asymmetry of Singapore's many skyscrapers quickly gives way to an urban cocktail of shops, temples and old colonial architecture. Whatever your view of this very modern city-state, there can be no doubt that it is a commercial success – a model of sustainable cosmopolitan capitalism for other aspiring economic centers such as Dubai. Lee Kwan Yew, Singapore's first prime minister after independence from British colonial rule in 1957, played a major role in creating this economic success story. His particular brand of leadership enabled a radical fusion of Asian values and Western capitalism that fueled and energized the economy to succeed beyond the possible limitations of its relatively minuscule size. Yew remained prime minister until 1990, but retained a politically idiosyncratic position as "Minister Mentor" even after stepping down. His success has been regarded as the result of strong intelligence, authoritarianism and personal charisma. But what is this "charisma" that people refer to when discussing leaders such as Lee Kwan Yew? Is it some sort of secret aspect of the human psyche that all leaders possess, or is it a mirage we conjure for ourselves to explain how others become successful? In short, is charisma attribute or attribution?

Charisma and attributes

Max Weber[16] is regarded as one of the founders of modern sociology. By all accounts, he was a precocious child: In 1876, at the age of thirteen, his Christmas gift to his parents consisted of historical essays charting the course of German history. Weber's interest in history persisted, but diversified into sociological and economic themes during later life. Weber's academic scholarship led him to develop a particular view of charisma and he defined it as

> a certain quality of an individual personality, by virtue of which s/he is "set apart" from ordinary people and treated as endowed with supernatural, superhuman, or at least specifically exceptional powers or qualities. These as such are not accessible to the ordinary person, but are regarded as divine in origin or as exemplary, and on the basis of them the individual concerned is treated as a leader.[17]

There is no ambiguity here: for Weber, charisma is an innate quality, real and powerful that marks an individual from the crowd. Notwithstanding Weber's recognized expertise and scholarship, his approach is no more than descriptive, a forerunner of the modern tendency to lapse into mysticism. Professor Richard Wiseman, at the University of Hertfordshire, has a more precise definition and proposes that charismatic people can induce their own emotions, such as excitement and enthusiasm, in others. He is leading an experiment with Channel 4 to explore this viewpoint.[18] The experiment involves two tracks of data collection: the first online and the second face-face. Web-users who participate are asked to rate the perceived charisma of eighteen would-be science presenters – not necessarily a field with which we might instantly associate this subject. The ratings are based solely on their appearance in photographs. The second stream of data comes from a team of judges evaluating charisma after a presentation on a science topic of preference chosen by one of the aspiring presenters. While the panel of judges based their ratings on a "range of information, including, for example, the applicants' facial looks, their clothes, body language and the way they spoke, as well as the content of their presentation," the online assessors had only photographic stills from which to make their initial evaluation. The initial results are fascinating: despite a gulf in the quality and depth of information used by the two groups to evaluate charisma, there is a very high degree of agreement. Wiseman interprets these results as suggesting charisma capability may be the result of either attractiveness, expressiveness of facial expressions or a combination of both.

Wiseman's work chimes with the earlier findings of Professor Friedman at the University of California. Based on a range of experiments designed to understand facial expressions, the communication of emotion and charisma, Professor Friedman has developed a test that, according to his personal web site, provides a measure of personal charisma. His Affective Communication Test does appear to have some validity. People who scored high on this test were paired with low scorers and placed in a room together. They were barred from talking and subsequently asked questions about their feelings. He found that in the briefest of periods, two minutes to be precise, the moods of the low scorers were influenced by those of the high scorers. Malcolm Gladwell, in *The Tipping Point*,[19] describes such results as demonstrating the contagious nature of emotions, and a basis for enthusing others. Charisma may indeed be gifted to a lucky few either by nature or nurture or a combination of both.

But how do we know *what* emotion is being communicated by one of these "emotional radiators"? For our own feelings to change and be in psychological sync with such people, we have to know what emotion they are "emitting." Charles Darwin became interested in this question and poured his thoughts into "The expression of emotions in man and animals." Over the years, psychologists have taken these ideas and subjected them to rigorous and inventive experiments. Paul Ekman, an American psychologist and a world-renowned expert in the field of emotions, found evidence of universal emotions that can be recognized independently of culture.[20] His classic work simply involved showing photographs of facial expressions to individuals from different cultures and asking them to identify which emotion they saw. Ekman reports that "observers in five different cultures gave the same interpretation of each face." His studies provide the basis for believing that these universal emotions form the lingua franca of charismatic individuals.

But there is a twist to this emotional tale. Ekman and his colleagues recognized that while emotions may be universal, general observation and common sense suggests that the way in which they are expressed and displayed does vary across cultures. To get to the heart of the matter, they intentionally contrasted emotional display rules with two very different cultures: American and Japanese. Their experiment involved an individual (either Japanese or American) sitting alone in a room watching either positive images of natural scenery or negative films of surgical procedures. A hidden video camera recorded the facial expressions, and subsequent analysis revealed "nearly identical muscle movement at nearly identical moments of the film." So far, so universal: cultural factors did not appear to play a role. However, in the second part of the experiment, the psychologists brought another person into the room – a Japanese scientist in Tokyo and an American one in Berkeley. Subsequent measurement of facial movements showed no correlation between Japanese and American individuals participating – cultural rules governing the display of emotion had now taken over and masked the fundamental nature of emotions. In other words, the language of emotion is universal, with basic building blocks hardwired into facial expressions. Later in our lives, cultural factors go to work in terms of determining how, in certain situations, these basic emotions are expressed. This leaves the road open for charismatic individuals to "infect" others with their own feelings, regardless of culture or experience; although we may not recognize the nature of that emotional impact until some time later. Still, charisma, in the more operational sense defined by Wiseman and Friedman, may just be cross-cultural – a finding that may go some way to explaining the global appeal of many leaders such as Nelson Mandela and Mahatma Gandhi.

To sum up the argument so far: the evidence seems to suggest that if we regard "charisma" as some form of highly effective communication of emotions, then it seems fair to draw the conclusion that charisma is a personal attribute – and one that we may or may not have. Looking at the data from an evolutionary perspective (often but not always a great litmus test of psychological hypotheses) would seem to indicate that this line of thinking makes sense: after all, our ability to emote predates our ability to speak; some of the most ancient areas of the brain are associated with emotions. Perhaps long ago, on the savannah of our ancestors, a time without words, grammar or syntax, perhaps then the power of emotional communication provided a means to survive longer than our competitors in that unforgiving landscape.

So, is charisma something that is passed on via our genes, or is it something we can learn? The story is not so simple. Trying to understand the nature of charisma from an attribution perspective gives us a different view of the issue.

Charisma and attributions

Georg Simmel is a writer and thinker who was born into this world at the hub of the economic epicenter of nineteenth-century Germany: Berlin.[21] His birthplace, the corner of Leipzigerstrasse and Friedrichstrasse, was a major crossroads in Berlin, at a time when the industrial revolution was expanding the economy and population of the city dramatically. Simmel wrote and lectured on a range of subjects, including psychology, economics, history and philosophy; although it is in the field of sociology that he left an indelible mark. He introduced the term "social distance" in an essay called "The Stranger," a short reflection that considers the impact of industrial progress on personal identity in a changing world. Simmel recognized how social distance – a measure of familiarity and connectedness – has a dynamic impact on social relations. In more recent times, researchers in the leadership field have come to recognize how social distance is an important lens through which we regard our leaders.

During the reign of Louis XIV, the Duke of Conde was reported as saying, "no man is a hero to his valet." His point is that the up close and personal relationship between a man and his valet in those by-gone times undermines any opportunity for the sense of mystique that is the source of our perception of charisma – so here charisma is an attribution, rather than an attribute. In Simmel's terminology, the short social distance mediates the nature of the relationship and determines how we perceive someone and the attributions we make about their character. In 1995, Shamir, an Israeli psychologist demonstrated that what is perceived as constituting a "charismatic leader" is partially a function of social distance.[22] Shamir's team asked 160 students to describe the characteristics of a leader that they knew directly, and another 160 to describe the charismatic characteristics of a leader with whom they did not have a direct relationship. The results indicated that distant leaders were "more frequently characterized as having rhetorical skills, having an ideological orientation and a sense of mission." In contrast, close leaders were characterized as being "more sociable, open, considerate and having a sense of humour." Exactly what constituted charisma was never defined for the subjects; the participating students were free to impose their own definition. Shamir's work indicates that social distance impacts on not whether or not someone is seen as charismatic, but on what sort of behaviors and characteristics are regarded as charismatic. In this sense, "charisma" may best be described as an interpretive label projected onto someone's behavior depending on the how we perceive them. *Charisma is not embedded in the individual but in our perception of that individual.*

But why should we project these characteristics onto people? Why should we infer that someone is charismatic? In truth, no one knows exactly. But we offer two possible explanations. Firstly, we are a social species and we learn about ourselves in a significant way by comparing ourselves to other people; psychologists call this the social comparison theory. If someone is perceived to be more successful than ourselves, for example, an admired CEO of a major organization, we need an explanation for the difference in our success. Charisma is one, easy option to explain why someone else has, in our eyes, achieved more than we have. In the absence of any notion of charisma, what other explanations are there? Good fortune? This may be true, but it does not appeal to our need for a rational and predictable world. More hardworking than us? Greater ambition? More drive? These explanations are also unpalatable because it suggests that the cause for our own relative lack of success may lie in our own hands: best to beatify others than to blame ourselves.

Our second reason is simple. Sometimes we all need heroes to make sense of our world for us; to make it seem a fairer, more just and more predictable world. Take Rudolf Giuliani. In the middle of 2001, *Time* magazine was ready to write him off. They described him pre-9/11 as a man "paddling off into oblivion with all the other lame ducks." In their end-of-year issue, they proclaimed him "Man of the Year: A tower of strength." There can be no doubt that Giuliani offered great leadership in New York's worst crisis. However, if it had not been for the dramatic and tragic shift in context, he would have been thrown onto the scrap heap of forgotten American politicians. When confronted with an uncertain and threatening world, we may not feel that we have control over our world, but it is comforting to believe that someone else does. What this also tells us is that when we are considering our leaders and their context, we should remember that we are not impartial observers. Our own context shapes the way we perceive the world and the people in it.

Finally, then, charisma is clearly a mixed and muddled concept: sometimes invoked to describe the attributes of individuals, it is equally likely to most accurately capture the attributions we make of others. In some situations, it is both.

CONCLUSIONS

At one level, this chapter has been about highlighting the pitfalls of what might be described as the seductive, commonsense view of leadership. It's a viewpoint that tries to distil the essence of leadership into a limited number of critical attributes, regardless of immediate organizational context and wider social and economic setting. Common sense has a track record for pulling the proverbial wool over our eyes. Einstein viewed common sense as no more than "the collection of prejudices by the age of eighteen." This chapter has tried to challenge our commonsense view of leadership. We have argued that the source of the leadership illusion, whether we are overly focused on the personality of the individual or fall into the trap of mystifying what leadership is all about or project character traits onto others as a means to explain our own position in the world relative to others, the common thread is failure to give sufficient credit to the importance of context *as well as* the individual.

In this book, we will talk about the leader in context. We will make a specific argument about the broader social, economic and organizational context that will have significant implications for the selection and development of leaders in the public sector, the private sector and in the wider political arena. In brief, that argument about context is simple: we live in an age in which the power of networks is just beginning to be felt. Understanding the nature and potential of networks, in all their guises, within and between organizations, across a daunting array of geographies and cultures, is, and will continue to be, central to successful leadership. The notion of the leadership illusion should remind us not to forget the context in which leaders operate, and of the need to consider the ideas, people and organizations that form those networks.

At the beginning of this chapter we discussed how, in 1915, Einstein's General Theory of Relativity lifted the veil on a more connected world than anyone had previously imagined. It's worth revisiting some of Einstein's thoughts in order to prepare ourselves for the rest of our leadership journey. He had this to say about our universe:

> Physical objects are not in space, but these objects are spatially extended (as fields). In this way the concept "empty space" loses its meaning. ... The field thus becomes an irreducible element of physical description, irreducible in the same sense as the concept of matter (particles) in the theory of Newton.[23]

If we can take the liberty of rephrasing one of the greatest minds of the twentieth century, it will enable us to set the tone for the rest of this book:

Leaders are not independent entities. Leaders do not exist by them-selves in organizational space, but are spatially extended (through their networks). In this way the concept "individual leader" loses its meaning. ... The network thus becomes an irreducible element of physical description.

Leaders and their networks is what this book is really about. It refuses to succumb to the fundamental driver underpinning the leadership illusion: the need for simple answers that fit into neat little conceptual boxes. The result might be a little messier than we like, but will be all the more honest and clear-sighted as a consequence.

2

OUR CONNECTED WORLD

The world is a messy place. That does not make adaptation and anticipation easy for leaders. Despite the hopes of the 1990's, hopes for a simpler, more unified world in which "East versus West" and "Communism versus Capitalism" were competing philosophical and economic schisms that would no longer be relevant to the geopolitical landscape, our planet has become increasingly and confusingly complex. We are faced with a dynamic and uncertain world where the global financial markets have collapsed in a shockingly precipitous fashion, in which terrorism has become a global enterprise, where unknown Russian oil magnates can buy iconic British football clubs outright and J. K. Rowling, a writer of children's books, has gone, in the space of about five years, from an unknown author, living in a one bedroom flat in Edinburgh, to one of the richest storytellers the world has ever seen. Who could have anticipated any of that? But amidst the apparent chaos and complexity at a global level, there are patterns and structures that have real implications for leaders.

The unpredictability of the world, the sheer, staggering pace of change ("business at the speed of thought," according to Bill Gates[1]) and the consequent complexity is fueled through a bemusing interplay of political, social, economic and technological forces. These factors combine together in a way that more often than not beats the "futurologists," those people who make a living from trying to imagine and predict the shape and form of this new world. Some have argued that mass air travel, through the increased interchange of people and ideas around the world, would provide the basis for a more stable planet. This is an imagined world where the sharing of people and information provides the basis for greater understanding and empathy on a global basis. Instead, the last decade has seen a rise of new insularities and divisions based on political nationalism, economic iniquities and/or religious fundamentalism. In part, this is due to the fact that the interchange of people, ideas and opportunity has only raised the realization of the inequalities that exist around the world. Economists in certain quarters have pointed out that about 300 individuals in the world receive the same total income as the other 3 billion people across the planet. This sort of materialistic Grand Canyon doesn't exactly encourage empathy and only serves to reinforce the feeling of unfair distribution of resources around our small world.

Nevertheless, it's difficult to get away from the fact that the movement of people around the world has increased dramatically in recent years. Urry, in his book *Global Complexity*, states that *"there are 700 million international journeys made each year"* and that this figure is expected to exceed one billion in the near future.[2] Whether the global recession and the impassioned arguments of the environmental lobby will have any impact on the aviation industry and these trends remains to be seen.

When people do travel, they don't go empty handed. In this case, they carry with them, either explicitly or implicitly, the cultural and social mores of their country of origin. They also take with them their own personal networks, invisible lines of connection that stretch across the world and mesh with new networks of peoples and cultures. Increasingly, these global networks are shaped and formed through religious or economic identity rather than national or geographical influences, but they have in common the breaking down of traditional geographical and political boundaries.

The potential for geographical mobility of this magnitude to have significant and unpredictable social and economic impact is given further impetus by the explosion of information technology advances, together with the improving access to this technology. You might imagine schools in rural Uganda to be hot and crowded with enthusiastic students who make the most of basic learning materials. Yet as long ago as 2005, at a school in Bugulumbya in rural Uganda, children were excitedly watching their favorite football teams on computers linked to the Internet. It was part of a program to bring technology to classrooms across the country. And it doesn't stop in Uganda. Have a look at the following website: www.laptop.org. This organization, One Laptop per Child Association, chaired by the digital guru Nicholas Negroponte, is dedicated to giving the world's poorest children access to a laptop with Internet connectivity and the kind of software that will transform how they will connect and collaborate with other children and adults, and radically enhance their opportunity for self-development.

This level of accessibility coupled with technological connectivity such as the World Wide Web and handheld, wireless computing have led some authors to talk about the "death of distance." This may seem a little far-fetched for those of us who have had frustrated experiences of using videoconferencing facilities; but it is true to say that individuals from radically different walks of life, frequently living thousands of miles apart, who, until a very few years ago, would never have come across each other, now communicate with ease in cyberspace – a virtual location where both time and distance is proving irrelevant. These new forms of social networks are shaped through a variety of mutual interests, from online gaming to building political capital, but, again, they breach the divides that have constrained human contact for thousands of years.

Perhaps one of the most striking examples of this is the virtual world of Second Life.[3] Created by Linden Labs, and physically located in a variety of offices across the United States, Second Life has all the wonders and vices of the real world. People interact with each other using avatars (computer generated characters) that are created by the user to varying levels of detail in terms of physical appearance and dress. But don't be fooled into thinking that Second Life is a gigantic, idle-chat room. There is a thriving business community in Second Life where all sorts of goods and services can be purchased using "Linden Dollars," purchased with "real money" using your credit card. And like all products of the human mind, this cyber market has both the innocently playful and the darkly perverse; beautiful parks, vibrant dance rooms and more than a few sex clubs that cater for every taste you can imagine, and possibly a few you can't. Increasingly, Second Life is being used by large organizations for more and more business uses, marketing products, conferences and education. Ultimately, Second Life is a rich source of connections and relationships that have never before been possible.

Perhaps nowhere is the emerging importance of our interdependent and newly connected lives quite as acute and impactful to us personally as in the so-called "networked, global economy." Manuel Castells is a multilingual, globe-trotting Professor at Berkeley who has more than a few things to say about our world and its networks. He maintains that this global economy was not created by markets, but through "the interaction between markets and governments and financial institutions acting on behalf of markets."[4] In other words, our global economy is a complex network of individuals, institutions and governments acting within a web of interdependence.

Of course, this economic network manifests itself both positively and negatively. If Jeff Skilling was the "canary in the cage" in 2001 for endemic corruption of organizations and their leaders in the near future, then the Asian market tumble in the latter stages of the twentieth century was an equivalent warning for the systemic, global collapse in 2009. In 1997, Thailand's financial crisis triggered another in Korea later in that same year. The knock-on effects, moving through the connections of the global economy, adversely impacted the economy of Russia in 1998 and, later in 1999, Brazil. Despite the fact that, as one commentator pointed out, "these countries have little in common, yet the financial crisis ... propagated from one to the next like a virus because of the links created by the global economy."

It must take some shock to move a British prime minister (of Scottish descent) to cite poetry, and English poetry to boot. Perhaps it was the unseasonably cold weather in Delhi during January 2008; though it may have been the early chill of an impending global recession. Whatever the inspiration, while speaking at the India-UK Business Summit, Gordon Brown reminded the audience of the words from the seventeenth-century poet John Donne: "no man is an island." While at the time, the prime minister may have been referring to the common problems India and the UK share around the world, he could easily have been talking about the world's banks: "no bank is an island, entire of itself. Each is a part of the continent, a part of the main." More recently, Great Britain's prime minister has warmed to the theme. In the midst of the 2009 financial meltdown, he stated, "in our interconnected global financial system, banks in any one country are often affected more by their international exposures to America and elsewhere than by any domestic defaults." This lottery of linkages across the banking system is a central, unarguable reason for the speed of the recent economic unraveling of our global economy.

These interconnections are not just a matter of dollars, sterling or yen. They are not about the ability of computers to think and communicate faster. At the heart of these financial links is a singular human emotion: trust. During the calamitous crash of company shares and house prices, employment and GDP in the latter phases of 2008 and early 2009, the crucial element has been the desperate erosion of trust and confidence between banks and their borrowers, and perhaps more critically between the banks themselves. The networks, the relationships and the emotions that make those networks thrive or dive, are all part of the modern leader's accountability.

One might reasonably anticipate that an awareness of the fragile interdependency of the global economy might have created a drive for a more multilateral leadership style. Some observers expected that, post-9/11, the United States would have led the way in global effort of network leadership in order to, as Will Hutton described it in 2002, "re-engage with the world as it sought to build and sustain a global coalition against terrorism."[5] It's up to the reader to decide whether or not "network leadership" of this sort has been apparent at a global level. What is certain is that the rapidly shifting lines of global connections between economies, people and information may change and morph, but they won't go away. Companies may be tempted to retreat into the relative safety of their own commercial backyard and countries may be seduced into short-term protectionist policies, but global networks will not disappear. In summary, the world may seem a messy place, but beneath the chaos is the subtle order and structure of a latticed world. People and places are linked together through networks that have recurring characteristics amidst the complexity, patterns that are understandable and there to be exploited by the alert and canny leader.

ORGANIZATIONAL NETWORKS

The world might seem chaotic, but in contrast organizations are presented as structures of order and routine. The boxes and neatly drawn lines of organizational charts are a man-made illusion that ignore the underlying web of relationships, the shifting sands of human connection that really hold the hidden secret of organizational success. The concept of networks and the implications for the achievement of organizational goals have been more obvious targets for network analysis and thought. Traditionally, this approach has tended to polarize at different ends of the corporate spectrum. For some writers, networks are only relevant to highly variable, unpredictable industries such as biotechnology or fashion, while for others the network concept is a key focus for large, multinational companies. However, we regard the network concept as being fundamental to a range of organizations, regardless of size or function. In the next few pages, we will set out our arguments on why we believe networks are universally important to all organizations.

There are numerous factors that underpin the relevance of networks to today's organizations. These factors can be separated conceptually, but in reality are very often interlocking facets of modern organizations. These factors include

- the increasing demands and risks of operating in a global marketplace, which drive the need to form connections and manage interdependencies across economies and countries;
- a drive for greater levels of innovation throughout organizations, regardless of sector or size;
- the arrival of the knowledge economy and the importance of the "informational advantage" for organizations;
- a drive to build supply chain networks that create the opportunities for partnerships and trade-offs in order to meet customer demands; and
- an increasing body of literature which demonstrates that high performance organizations are also characterized by the high involvement of its employees.

In all five factors, the old-fashioned hierarchical structure of an organization with its fixed lines of top-down communication, traditional functional units with carefully defined, bounded roles for individuals, present more of a hindrance than a help to organizations trying to develop and sustain these factors. Why? Because the deployment of traditional hierarchy makes three moribund assumptions:

- Your competitive context is stable and that consequently any competitive pressures are both manageable and, indeed, knowable;
- The processes which underpin an organization are regular and stable;
- The output of any organization, be it service, product or concept, is fixed and determined by the organization rather than "consumers."

The traditional hierarchy and its related assumptions implicitly view the world as existing within a "push" rather than "pull" economy. A "push" economy assumes it can anticipate end-user demands and brings together materials and people, typically in a single location, to create products and services that meet those demands. A "push" economy is typified by the mode of production and economic structure in the nineteenth and twentieth centuries. Conversely, the "pull" economy is user-centric and market-centric rather than product-centric, recognizes that often end-user demand may be unpredictable and requires organizational structures and processes that are flexible and frequently decentralized. An organization typical of the push economy is characterized by bureaucracy, while an organization of the pull genre is characterized by enterprise.

While much attention has been paid to the rational design of organizations for optimal performance, too little attention has been paid to the sort of leadership behaviors that enable more complex organizational designs, particularly based on a pull business model, to really work.

Let's just take a few minutes to flesh out those factors in more detail in order to understand more clearly why hierarchy and simple structural divisions are inadequate for the challenges in the twenty-first century.

1 Risk and global markets

Although we discussed this earlier, we want to return to this theme from the perspective of anticipating and managing risk within the global market. In the past, most business leaders recognized, at least in principle, that risk involves analyzing three central factors of politics, economics and finance. Although, today, it is apparent that there is another factor that organizational leaders should consider when making bold decisions that are cognizant of any concomitant risk: the environmental factor. This factor includes availability of natural resources, as well as climate-related issues.

In most organizations, however, an understandable drive for simplicity across these four broad factors often results in this data becoming aggregated in such a way that final information, critically relevant to effective commercial decisions, is lost or ignored. It is the careful synthesis of all strands of information that is important. However, in the hypersensitive global economy, a business leader needs to consider these factors across a range of countries, and possibly markets, in order to make the best possible decisions. There has to be a constant struggle to balance the needs of the whole organization and the demands of the local market place. This cannot be achieved through a classic, hierarchical structure in which information flow is typically from the Board downward and in which information is gradually filtered and processed on its way back to the centralized decision maker at head office. Consequently, organizational structures need to reflect this need. However, beyond structure, the underlying relationships – the networks across countries, markets and business units – have to drive the success of that structure.

2 Drive for innovation

Everyone needs to innovate. Although some say that innovation is really the "raison d'etre" of the multinational corporation, it is true to say that every organization today strives in some way, shape or form to be more innovative. Whether you are a global manufacturer, a university, a biotechnology company in Cambridge or one of the so-called Silicon Alley companies in New York, innovation is the key to creating value and staying competitive. However, contrary to contemporary myth, innovation is not something that happens in glorious isolation. Researchers today recognize the importance of networks, at an organizational or individual level, for encouraging innovation in all its forms. Innovation is a team sport!

At MIT, Eric Von Hippel researches and advocates the "democratization" of innovation.[6] Users, aided by improvements in computer and communications' technology, increasingly can develop their own new products and services. These innovating users – both individuals and firms – often freely share their innovations with others, creating user-innovation communities and a rich source of common intellectual property.

The leadership challenge for organizations that embrace an outside-in, collective approach to innovation is quite different from those that operate an inside-out, functional process for innovation.

3 The knowledge advantage

"Knowledge is the battlefield for countries, corporations and individuals," so wrote the unorthodox and engaging authors of *Funky Business* published in 1999.[7] They argue persuasively that "knowledge really is power"; certainly, in the complex and competitive society we have been discussing, knowledge and its necessary corollary – understanding – would seem critical to our collective and individual success.

However, it would seem that knowledge is not enough. An old jazz musician once said about his profession that "knowledge and ideas are cheap, it's putting them into practice that's hard." It would seem the same is true of organizations.

Pfeffer and Sutton wrote,

> Why [do] so many managers know so much about organisational performance, say so many things about how to achieve performance, and work so hard yet are trapped in firms that do so many things they know will undermine performance?[8]

These authors argue that knowledge is not enough by itself because frequently there is a gap, if not a chasm, between the "knowing" and the "doing." How do organizations transmute base knowledge into organizational gold? How is this relevant to our network perspective? One of the most critical factors emerging from Pfeffer & Sutton's analysis of organizations that manage to bridge the knowing-doing divide is that they work at building communities of practice in which people share ideas and thoughts and then work hard collectively at transferring knowledge into real day-to-day behaviors. The sort of culture required to achieve this develops webs of practitioners who are not afraid to experiment, make mistakes, ask what appears to be the stupid question, and then share that experience with each other.

4 Supply chain networks

The supply chain concept is radically changing the way that organizations do business. To cope with the increasing demands of globalization, organizations are being forced to consider trade-offs between inventory costs, transports costs and response time to the customer. Rather than conceptualizing the link between the organization and its customers as being a linear process from manufacturing to delivery at point-of-sale, or point-of-sale back to manufacturing, many organizations recognize the complex network of suppliers, partners, clients and customers with the requisite complexity of interactions and interdependencies these networks create.

One contemporary example of an organization successfully implementing an effective network organization based on a "pull" rather than push business model is the Li & Fung clothing company in China. Li & Fung has only 500 employees, but has a network of over 7500 business partners internationally. Hagel and Brown (2005) state that LI & Fung "mobilizes this broader network to customize specific global supply networks for its customers ... Given the specific product and service requirements of individual customers, this company assembles the right business partners to meet demanding cost, quality and timing specifications. It can rapidly move specific business partners in and out of the supply networks to adapt to changing customer needs or market conditions. The success of this model can be seen in its performance figures: the company generates over $5 billion in revenue – over $1 million per employee – and 30 to 50 percent return on equity."[9]

5 High performance, high involvement organizations

Over the last eight years, there have been several studies, across a number of different sectors that have highlighted the importance of building highly interactive groups of employees for organizational effectiveness. This should come as a surprise to no one, but finally there is hard data to support the commonsense view. These studies, for example, Huselid in 1997[10] consistently demonstrate that the most important factor for predicting organizational success along a broad set of metrics is the presence or absence of people-related practices designed to build individual capability and social capital. The most recent of these studies, Thompson (2002),[11] carried out in the highly competitive aerospace sector, found that high performance practices increased retention of key performers, led to an average sale per employee 161 percent higher than comparable organizations without these practices.

A new perspective on high-performance organizations in the UK has been afforded by research from The Work Foundation in the UK with organizations of all shapes and sizes.[12] This study, conducted over a period of eighteen months, found very similar results to previous high-performance studies, but identified one critical factor not explored in earlier work. Their work suggests that perhaps the most critical, overriding factor for engendering high performance is the ability of an organization to operate cross-functionally and to manage successfully the trade-offs generated by the interdependencies across the organization. However, high performance, high involvement organizations, whether in the private or the public sectors, do not come about without a leader who demonstrates sensitivity and awareness to organizational networks. One such leader is Eric Thomas, Vice Chancellor of Bristol University.

We first met Eric a couple of years ago when commissioned to conduct research focusing upon the challenges facing Vice Chancellors and their equivalents within UK Universities. With a remit to identify the attributes that best equip them for meeting those challenges, we were immediately struck by Eric's frequent reference to the value of his numerous contacts and relationships across a wide range of academic, professional and community groups. He spontaneously referenced these as he described how he tackles the complex challenges that he faces in his role, but also acknowledged that this value is not recognized by all of his academic colleagues.

I operate in an internal environment where **what you know** – your academic prowess, professional standing and expert reputation, have historically defined your sense of identity and self-worth. As a researching, publishing and teaching academic this is no bad way of benchmarking your success and value – both within your organisation, and more widely within your area of specialism and expertise. But then we frequently call upon these same individuals to undertake significant leadership roles within our institutions. This can mean across departments, across disciplines and in the case of Vice Chancellor, even across the many social, economic and political entities that form a city like Bristol. That's when true leadership is less about you, and more about those that you represent, those that you need to know, and ultimately, those that you can genuinely connect and work with.

Eric is well qualified to comment upon this shift of leadership perspective. His earlier leadership roles included Head of the School of Medicine and then Dean of the Faculty of Medicine, Health and Biological Sciences at Southampton University. Both while continuing to practice as a consultant gynaecologist. The change from this specialist focus to the full remit of the leadership of Bristol University was, reflects Eric, a very significant one.

From his uncluttered, unpretentious office (none of the oak-paneled walls, gilt-framed oils or leather-bound tomes that define the territory of his counterparts in equally prestigious "ivory towers"), Eric looks out of the wide picture windows at the City of Bristol that forms both the backdrop, and the heart, of his particular leadership challenge. His love for his university is inextricably linked to his love for the city in which it resides, prospers and ultimately depends. This interdependency was one of the first "breakthrough moments" that Eric had upon his appointment in 2001. He gave as an example a particularly sensitive application by the university to develop buildings that had a significant impact upon the city center landscape. He recognized the need to maintain an open and honest dialogue with the leader of the City Council throughout the early planning and application stages. While recounting this episode he is adamant about the integrity of these conversations.

> I know that this may be viewed cynically as "pulling strings at the top." But it's not. It's about sharing intention, aspiration and purpose in a human, genuine way.

Questioned about how he demonstrates the genuineness of his relationships he answered instantly:

> I don't lie. When I say it, I mean it. We have to search for solutions that are best for everybody, that add substantial value to all sides. That can only be achieved by being there, making sure that you have your say, and also listening just as hard as you speak.

Eric has no doubt about the importance of communication, not just with those of equivalent authority and responsibility, but with everyone with whom he comes in contact.

> A good measure of this is can you, and **do you want to**, understand how that person sees the world? The same applies to everyone I meet, whether they are a dignitary, receptionist, Minister or student. Whatever the event, you **do** need to introduce yourself, and if you don't know who they are you must instantly be honest, apologise and ask. I have learnt painfully on occasion, never to make assumptions about people having met them. You can never know everything about a person, and you can certainly never know who they may become and how you may be able to help each other in the future.

Talking us through a typical week in his diary, it becomes evident that Eric spends a vast amount of his time representing his university, his city and even his country at seemingly endless meetings, social functions and other formal events. He agrees that you do have to enjoy this aspect of the Vice Chancellor role in order to be truly effective.

> Fundamentally, you have to be interested in what people have to say. Of course you are there for a reason, but so are they. Find out what that reason is and you can be amazed by how it impacts, complements and frequently strengthens your own position.
> "And if it doesn't?" He grinned:
> "Well then, you certainly needed to know that sooner rather than later!"

Although our original connection with Eric came through his role as Vice Chancellor of Bristol University, having spent a little time mapping his Social Network with him, the extent of his involvement and reach, not just within the UK, but internationally becomes evident. For example, he has recently held the Chair of the Worldwide Universities Network.

As with all our interviewees, we concluded the interview by asking Eric whether he knew of others within his network that he would consider to be "Network Leaders." Without hesitation he leafed through his mental address book, leaned forward and talked us through a veritable Who's Who of leaders, well outside that of a typical leader within the education sector. He spoke of each affectionately, in detail and urged us to contact them – with his regards and explicit referral. He was happy to guide us and support us in making further connections, but then, with complete trust allowed us to start our own exploration through his network without further attempt at control or interference.

So, from whatever perspective we decide to look at contemporary organizations, the network perspective has something to say about their design and structure. More importantly, in the context of this book, it sets out a new agenda for leadership that should be considered alongside this emerging organizational context.

PERSONAL NETWORKS

Networks of opportunity

The notion that there are "six degrees of separation" that connect us toanyone on the planet is an idea that has proved to be contagiously intriguing. John Guare, in his 1991 play *Six Degrees of Separation* highlighted the profound belief that everyone on the planet, from Presidents to Eskimos, natives in rain forests to gondoliers in Venice are connected by just six other people.[13] However, this notion isn't a new one. As long ago as 1929, a Hungarian writer, Karinthy, published a set of short stories, 52 in total (one for every week of the year) in which one story was called, quite simply: "Chains."[14] The leading character proposes that he can link himself to anyone on the planet – a global population of approximately one and a half billion at the time – through no more than five links. The protagonist proves his thesis by connecting himself to a Nobel Laureate. "Chains" is a story little known in the West and it was not until the early 1960's that this idea found a new voice and a new prominence through the social psychologist, Stanley Milgram.

Milgram is perhaps most famous, or infamous depending on your perspective, for conducting a never-repeated series of experiments on human obedience.[15] These inventive, if somewhat unethical experiments, involved unwitting volunteers who were asked to inflict increasingly severe electric shocks to "disobedient" volunteers who were seated in another room. In fact, the "disobedient volunteers" were actually in league with Milgram and the team of experimenters. They were not actually receiving shocks, but acted as if they were. Despite the apparent suffering of the "disobedient" ones, the real subjects of the experiment continued to inflict what they thought to be severe electric shocks at the request of a man in a white coat with a serious looking clipboard. The point of the experiment, according to Milgram, is that all it takes is an authority figure, and our tendency to comply will manifest itself. The experiment continues to generate controversy today,[16] but, if nothing else, demonstrated Milgram's knack for choosing psychological topics that catch the eye.

In the 1960's, Milgram decided to conduct an experiment to study scientifically the degrees of separation hypothesis, or the "small world problem," as it was known at this time.[17] A perfect example of the small world problem occurred while one of us was in a local Cornwall pub, eating a meal and writing some of this chapter. Two "random" couples began talking to each other on the basis that they each had Border Terriers. Once the conversation started rolling, it soon became clear that they were not only from the same county in England, but knew the same people in that county. "What a small world," they declared. Milgram's experiment set out to test whether or not our social worlds were, indeed, small.

Milgrams's experimental design involved handing out letters to a few hundred people in various areas across the United States. All of these letters had on them the name of the same stockbroker who lived in Boston, Massachusetts. The goal was to ensure that this letter arrived at its destination by passing it on to someone who may be more closely connected with the broker in Boston. Although we will consider the details of this experiment in a later chapter, Milgram found that, on average, the letter took six steps to arrive at its destination, hence the phrase "six degrees of separation." Milgram's work, although flawed, has caught on in many diverse ways, and set a trail that has led to more rigorous scientific models that have demonstrated the reality of the small world phenomenon.

Milgram's work began to point toward how closely we may be connected to other people. However, it is the diversity of our social networks that lead to the "new doors opening to other worlds." The Sociologist Granovetter has demonstrated this point elegantly in the early 1970's and captured it memorably with the phrase, *the strength of weak ties.*[18] His work showed that white-collar workers find jobs more effectively through acquaintances, or, in the parlance of social psychologists, people with whom we have weak ties; rather than people who we would consider as friends, or people with whom we have strong ties. Both Milgram and Granovetter led the way in helping people to recognize that understanding the characteristics of networks is useful for understanding and being more effective in our social worlds. In Chapter 4 we will consider more recent work on the nature of networks and their importance for effectiveness within and across organizations.

PARALLEL LIVES

Man has not one and the same life. He has many lives, placed end to end, and that is the cause of his misery.

Chateaubriand (eighteenth century)[19]

If only life were as simple as Chateaubriand's complaint. Contemporary living has changed beyond all recognition since that quote taken from the eighteenth century; it has changed substantially since

Granovetter's initial work on the strength of weak ties. Life, and work, today is no longer unilinear: it isn't laid out end to end, traveling in a single direction. Life happens in parallel. There is such a fusion, and confusion, between the public and the private, the organization and the home, work and play, customers and suppliers, clients and friends, that the old dichotomies are now rendered meaningless. We exist in a web of connections and possibilities created by those connections. Heidegger once said, "you are your projects."[20] Today, you are your network.

And why shouldn't life be like that? Gone are the times when you left school, chose your job, and stuck to it, until you shuffled off to your pension. Richard Reeves points out in *Happy Mondays*: "Workers in their fifties say that they have had four major jobs; workers in their thirties have already had that many. In the US, the average 32-year old worker has had nine jobs."[21]

These webs of connection, enabled by the technological advances described at the beginning of this chapter, mean that we can pursue multiple paths and develop multiple skills. We no longer need to be defined by a single job, no more than we need to be defined by the personality of a single friend. Careers experts have developed new language to describe this networked approach to our working lives: terms such as "zig zag" and "boundaryless" careers or "portfolio jobs" have emerged; while those who sometimes feel defensive about the experimental nature of their career "paths" describe them as "non-linear." John Stuart Mill, in a prescient remark, argued that we are not machines, but that we are like trees, "which require to grow and develop on all sides."[22] It's a useful and far-sighted metaphor that captures the organic network of our personal and working lives.

So what does it feel like to be embedded in the world pictured below (see Figure 2.1)? The truth is that while it brings individual and collective opportunity, it also brings tension, contradiction and conflict. "Work life balance" (WLB) is a term much in vogue; though the phrase is nebulous at the best of times. For some, WLB is a battle cry for a shorter working day and emancipation from the yoke of the oppressive and exploitative employer. For others, it means the freedom to commit every hour of every day to the profession of their choice. WLB, in our view, is all about freedom, flexibility and personal responsibility. The freedom to structure work in such a way as to balance the tensions and interdependencies inherent in the complex social structures in

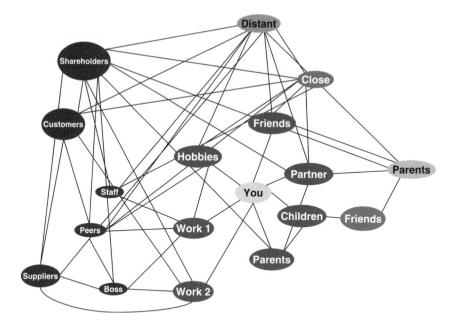

FIGURE 2.1 **Our networked lives**

which most of us live; flexibility to change our working patterns to find compromise and balance; and the personal responsibility to execute those choices in a way that maintains the integrity of the social, psychological and professional contracts that bind us into our network. WLB is leading and managing our complex interdependencies.

What implications do these personal networks have for leaders, or indeed anyone in organizations today? Firstly, we have to realize that it is not just our lives that are so complex, but also the lives of those people with whom we share our organizations. We may feel ourselves to be the center of our own web, but we are, at the same time and to different degrees, part of the networked worlds of others. Recognizing the opportunities and challenges that are part and parcel of those worlds places new demands on leaders, both in living and leading successfully.

THE CASE FOR NETWORK LEADERSHIP

Over the last twenty pages or so we have discussed the ubiquity of the network perspective. Whether we are considering the global, the

organizational or the personal, our postmodern lives can be characterized as being part of complex, networked social structures that contain
an inevitable level of complexity. That complexity creates a web of
interdependencies. Leaders for today and tomorrow will have to face
the complexity and those interdependencies with new approaches
and a different frame of mind. Those interdependencies bring with
them, often at the same moment, both opportunities and conflicts;
they demand more than simple command and control models of
leadership with straightforward binary win/lose solutions. Understanding the common characteristics of networks, and the behaviors
that underpin effective performance within and across networks will
be a central part of leadership for the twenty-first century. In the rest
of this book we hope to demonstrate that the network-perspective
is more than an "evocative metaphor" but provides a basis, albeit
dynamic, for the articulation of new principles of leadership through
the research and studies collated from a range of sources, researchers,
organizations and, most critically, *real* leaders in the world today.

3

THE RIGHT SORT OF
SOCIAL CAPITAL

OVERVIEW

Networks however are only a means to an end. It is the quality and the diversity of relationships within those networks – the social capital – that is the critical factor. Social capital is the currency that can make or break your organization. Forget about the vagaries, uncertainties and the complexities of financial capital. It's the ebb and flow of ideas and aspirations, commitment and collaboration (both inside and outside your organization) that create an invisible coinage, which differentiates successful organizations from the rest. That may seem to many readers to be a statement that is naïve at best and irresponsible at worst, given that it is written in early 2009, a time when the financial markets have imploded at a rate and scale not seen since the Great Depression of 1929. Our argument in the course of the next few pages is that it is exactly the *wrong* sort of social capital that has played such a significant role in the economic depression unraveling during 2008 and 2009.

If you think that the idea of "social capital" is something abstruse and academic, a fanciful flight for the fuzzy thinkers in organizational life, then think again. There are too many studies of high-performing organizations where the irresistible force is, neither technology nor products, but the capability and commitment of people. Every year in the United Kingdom, the *Sunday Times* publishes a survey of the Top 100 organizations that provides compelling evidence of the link between a socially rich, connected organization and success measured against a range of indicators, including customer satisfaction, profitability and share price.[1] Similarly, in 2005, The Work Foundation, a research organization based in London, went in search of the productivity gaps in UK-based companies. In a survey of over a 1000 organizations from a variety of sectors, it was the people factor that made the difference:

The key factor to executing the High Performance Index is the contribution of people. "Managing the spaces in-between" or integrating [across core areas], can only be achieved by a workforce that sees the big picture and is enabled and motivated to act, with middle managers able to translate strategy into workforce goals."[2]

Our central argument throughout this book is that the role of a leader is to develop the *right sort* of social capital (because not all social capital is good) both for their organizations and for themselves. Why? Because leaders do not achieve results on their own: building the right balance of relationships with others – and what constitutes "right" is context dependent – is critically important for leaders in the twenty-first century. To be honest, it's hard to imagine a time when this would not have been true.

The purpose of this chapter is practical. We want leaders to be more effective at developing social capital, both for themselves and for their organizations. To achieve that goal, both personally and organizationally, we believe it's important to understand what the term "social capital" actually means, in plain language, avoiding the loose analogies and misty semantics that often obscure the simple and straightforward meaning of the words. And having understood the terminology, then to come to grips with the mechanics and structural aspects of people networks. This will enable leaders to find new and practical ways to deliver the intangible and tangible benefits that social capital can offer.

THE SLIPPERY SLOPES OF SOCIAL CAPITAL

What is social capital – just a trendy new idea for the chattering classes to debate over lattes and cappuccinos in coffee bars around the world? The term certainly causes a lot of disagreement, and often not a little derision. At its core, the phrase refers to the *consequences* of social activity. Whether it's three people gathered around the hypothetical water cooler at the office chatting about last night's TV and building a sense of shared identity, or three hundred people at a political rally cheering their favorite candidate and demonstrating political solidarity, social capital is the invisible thread that binds people together for a variety of purposes. Why is it so important? We should never forget that human beings are a sociable lot and consequently relationships matter. And that's the essence of social capital: relationships do matter.

The quality and quantities of the connections between people enables us to take on tasks and challenges (and succeed) that are unlikely to be achieved independently. Our social networks provide the necessary conduit of connections through which social capital can flow. And from social capital, success.

However, at this point we need to sound the alarm. One of the reasons that this is such a slippery topic, both conceptually and practically, is that social capital can be understood at different levels of analysis, ranging from the societal to the individual. We can understand social capital from the perspective of

1. Society as a whole, e.g., the degree of fragmentation or cohesion in any social context;
2. An organization, e.g., the levels of collaboration and innovation across an organization;
3. The individual, e.g., the sum total of anyone's individual relationships across a social network.

For the next hundred pages or so, we focus on both individual leaders and organizations, but it is important to remember that both of these "levels" do not exist in a vacuum. Both the person and the organization are placed in, and affected by, a broader social context, which we always have to take into consideration. However, an awareness of levels of social capital is not the end of it. Even when we are aware of those different levels, its mercurial quality makes it difficult to nail down with any precision. Perhaps contemporary American sociologist Robert D. Putnam offers one of the simplest and most straightforward definitions of social capital:

> ... features of social life – networks, norms and trust – that enable participants to act together more effectively to pursue shared objectives.[3]

Putnam's definition is intuitive and alluring. If organizations are not about networks of people working together to achieve a common goal, what are they? Probably out of business or massively inefficient is the answer (and in today's unforgiving economy, the latter is no doubt a few, short steps from the former). However, day-to-day life in organizations tells us that while the words and the rhetoric about "trust" and "collaboration" may trip off the tongue easily, the reality is harder to create. Let's not underestimate the challenge to encourage people to work together in a collective spirit that supports the success of an organization. We have to get past individual differences in terms of personal ambition, focus and style; we have to explore and exploit the cultural chasms that may exist within and between organizations. In short, the language of "social capital" may appear simple, but the challenges it creates, both for organizations and their leaders, are not.

And aside from the "social" aspects of this term, what do we mean by "capital"? Are we referring to something that can be measured, invested and recouped in the same way as we might invest in a piece of machinery, a phase of R&D or the share price of a glittering prospect on the stock market? Or is it just a metaphor that emphasizes the importance of human relationships in language that accountants and their Chief Executives find comfortable? It's a tricky question. Some people feel that the word "capital" itself debases and dehumanizes the value of social activity. For others, there is no point talking about it if you can't measure it. Given the often polarized nature of this debate, it's worth understanding how the term "social capital" has evolved over the last forty or fifty years in order that leaders can truly appreciate the full implications for themselves and their organizations.

Will Hutton, journalist, economist, political commentator and CEO of the Work Foundation is a social capital enthusiast who turns fine rhetoric into hard reality. Ex-editor of the *Observer* newspaper, Mr Hutton is a leader who not only exemplifies how leaders can turn social capital to their own advantage, but who has a firm belief in the importance of this concept for the individual, for organizations and for society as a whole. Will Hutton is a network leader. We interviewed Will to map out his thoughts on social capital and how this idea has influenced his own success as a leader.

Six-foot-three and counting, Will arrived at least forty minutes late (not an unusual occurrence) in the trendy wine bar where we had agreed to meet, with a physically apparent and surprising diffidence created by his height and media profile. Some men stoop to conquer, Will Hutton stoops to connect. As a leader who has connected ideas and people across social and commercial divides, his intuitive development of his own social capital is a fundamental part of his success.

We started our interview with the simple question: "Will, what does the term social capital mean to you?"

"Social capital is the non-transactional, human dimension to relationships."

We pushed him to elaborate.

"Too often people just focus on the utilitarian aspects of interaction. They don't connect. They don't try to *really* understand each other."

Why is social capital important for organizations?

"For a start, it's important for the internal health of the organization. Social capital can give you shared norms and shared emotions. Mutual respect. And common purpose. When you're running an organization, you can't undervalue those things. But now it reaches way beyond the traditional internal structures of the organization. Ten years ago structure was a critical aspect of organizational success. It's still important, but not critical. Ten years ago, an organization's form and purpose were, generally speaking, clearly defined. That's not so true today. Today's organizations, the effective ones, are porous and struggle to continually redefine themselves. In some sectors they compete with organizations, and in others they may collaborate with those same people. Social capital is important because you never know when you might need it."

SOCIAL CAPITAL: A BRIEF REVIEW

By all accounts, French sociologist Pierre Bourdieu was a man of outspoken opinion who to all intents and purposes gave birth to the concept of social capital. Forty years ago he began a stream of work that examined the nature of culture, pursuing an argument that culture is both constantly changing and which simultaneously manages to retain some enduring structural elements over time.[4] His interest in these ideas stemmed from his desire to develop a form of sociological anthropology that explained status inequalities between people. For example, he created the term "cultural capital" and used it to try to explain the differences in educational outcomes in France during the 1960's. In particular, he believed he could explain such gaps as a function of differences in three forms of "capital": cultural, societal and economic. From his perspective, social capital interacts with the other two forms of capital as a form of "multiplier." Colorfully, in a radio interview in 1987, he argued that human beings gamble in the casino of social status with the red, black and green chips of these different aspects of capital available in society.

Despite the importance of social capital in his work, Bourdieu never developed its meaning with sufficient force and clarity. For him the term was no more than a useful concept that always remained secondary in its importance to the idea of cultural and economic capital, concepts he regarded as being more deserving of serious attention and research. Bourdieu also tended to view social capital as solely the property of elite groups, and failed to really consider that people in less fortunate situations might benefit from, or even have access to their own, social capital. Nevertheless, he established the concept as an idea that deserved more focused consideration.

If Bourdieu gave life to the concept of social capital, James Coleman nurtured the idea to maturity.[5] A distinguished American sociologist, Coleman brought his ideas to a much wider, typically English-speaking, audience than his French counterpart. He also approached the concept from a very different viewpoint. Where Bourdieu viewed the notion of social capital from an entirely social perspective, Coleman emphasized the importance of the individual. In the context of this book, Coleman's views and approach are much more relevant to our idea of network leadership.

Coleman's approach is dominated by a view of human beings that regards social interactions as a result of a series of rational choices. For Coleman, this perspective explained how people manage to co-operate, and derives from an overlap between economics and mathematics known as "Game Theory." A typical example of Game Theory is the "Prisoners' Dilemma."[6] In the Summer of 2008, Hollywood brought the Prisoner's Dilemma to life in the latest Batman movie: *The Dark Night*.[7]

The situation, for those that haven't succumbed to this dark rendering of the Batman story, was fiendishly simple. Two ferries set sail from Gotham city, fleeing from the latest act of anarchy perpetrated by the Joker, and heading for the other side of the river. One ferry is teeming with criminals from Gotham prison: the other is filled to the brim with "normal folk" – the men, women and children of Gotham. Unbeknownst to the passengers of either Ferry, the Joker had taken control of the ships remotely and placed enough explosives in the bowels of each ferry to level a city. The Joker had also placed a detonator on each ship – but it is the detonator for the explosives on the other Ferry. The choice is straightforward for the passengers: blow the other boat to smithereens and save yourself. Coleman's rational choice theory predicts that the only logical course of action is to get your hands on the detonator and throw the switch before you are sent to meet your maker. However, a sense of collective morality prevails on both boats and no one blows anyone up! In the movie, it seems a bit "cheesy" that this happens. But in real life, similar results are found with classical versions of the Prisoner's Dilemma.

In a more typical, hypothetical version of this moral conundrum, people are captured and put into cells in isolation from each other. They are told *individually* that if they offer a confession about the guilt of the other prisoner, then their own punishment will be mitigated. Each person is then confronted with a moral challenge – "fess up and mitigate your own punishment, or stay quiet in the hope that the other prisoner does the same," and possibly both parties walk away with no punishment at all, since there is no other evidence to convict them of the crime they are alleged to have committed.

Again, the problem is that rational choice theory predicts that a person will opt for a decision that will lead to the best result for them *individually*. In the Prisoners' Dilemma, there is no guarantee of co-operation from the other person. This means that the most rational, individual choice is to opt for a confession that improves their own situation but condemns the other person. Yet the results of simulations of the Prisoners' Dilemma, and more importantly real world events, tell us this isn't true: people make choices that are about collaboration and self-sacrifice all the time. Social capital is Coleman's conceptual "get out of jail" card. In his view, social networks and social norms allow for a collaborative choice to be "invested" for the future in anticipation of a later reward for the individual. In the Prisoners' Dilemma, the idea of social capital offers a clear rationale to opt for a more collaborative course of action. Teamwork, in this sense, is just a question of temporary sacrifice of our individual needs to meet the demands of the group in the expectation of some sort of payback at a later date.

Our work, our research and our practical experience have tossed up dozens of examples where leaders eschew the opportunity for immediate, individual gain and make sacrifices for the team and for the common good of the organization. In terms of the Prisoners' Dilemma, these leaders opt for a strategy of silence. Sometimes this behavior is the result of a conscious favor that they expect to be repaid at a later date; but for others, collaboration and personal sacrifice is an intuitive decision that in no way creates an expectation of some sort of social "credit." For these people, this is instinctive behavior that just feels right. We'll explore the benefits of this behavior, conscious or otherwise, in just a moment. But first, here are the views of Eric Thomas, Vice Chancellor of the University of Bristol about the notion of sacrifice and leadership.

> If it is good for the university, if it is good for Bristol, or if it is good for education **and** I have something to contribute or to learn – then I should be there. If it is also good for my career, then that's a bonus. There have been choices I have had to make, opportunities I have had to turn down, that may have advanced my career, but which would have severely distracted my attention from my commitment to my current role. Of course you think about that when you consider career moves, and that time will come again in due course. Right now my focus has to be upon what is good for the university and what is good for Bristol.

And so we come to James D. Putnam. This is the man who took the notion of social capital, and with some colorful imagery and provocative articles, sent it out into the world where the idea has developed a popular following. Such a popular following that in the late nineties Bill Clinton invited him to Camp David for a weekend of rustic political debate around the topic. Clinton's invitation to Putnam was a clear sign that social capital had graduated from the narrow and abstract world of sociological debate into the mainstream arena of politics and policy.

How does Putnam's view of social capital differ from Bourdieu and Coleman? How is it relevant to the world of twenty-first-century Leaders and their organizations? Putnam regards social capital as the "super glue" of effective social organization, and, in this sense, is useful for organizations specifically and society generally. From the Putnam perspective, social capital is what leaders develop for their organizations rather than for themselves.

His views stemmed from a decline in what he regarded as *civic engagement* in the United States. The example he uses to illustrate his point is the deterioration in the number of bowling teams and clubs across the United States. Bowling is seen by Putnam to be a classic example of what he terms "associational life" and, as such, is not just a hobby but a form of social activity that knits together the fabric of communities. In his book, *Bowling Alone*, he examines a range of social activities that have declined in recent years resulting in the fragmentation and dislocation of social life across the country.

Putnam's research establishes a compelling case that "features of social organization ... like trust ... and networks ... can improve the efficiency of society by facilitating co-ordinated actions." He goes on to argue that a lack of social capital can increase the possible "costs" for people who operate without those networks: What Putnam sees as important for society, is also true for organizations. If only Putnam's perspective told the whole story.

THE PROBLEM WITH PUTNAM

Ron Burt is the Professor of Sociology at the Chicago Booth School of Business. He is a charming, articulate individual with an unusual handshake. Whether he is meeting you for the first time or not, when he shakes hands with you, he takes your hand in a firm grip, then places his other hand over the two clasped hands, in a gesture that seems to bless the new connection with real sincerity and significance. Whether it's deliberate or not, it is disarming. It may be no coincidence that his Father was a priest. Aside from his engaging approach to meeting people, he is also ferociously bright with one of those intellects that seems to glide over a range of topics with ease. For some time now, he has been applying that brainpower to understanding social capital both academically and practically. Over the last few years, Professor Burt has been evangelizing an important distinction in the world of social capital, a view that is enormously important if we are to derive practical application for organizations and leaders, and which is the final stop in our journey to understand the development of social capital.

"Brokerage" and "closure" are the terms that Professor Burt has coined to underscore a fundamental distinction for social capital.[8] Let's start with closure. When social capital is characterized by closure, it results from the trust and strong social norms advocated by Putnam. Closure is at its most beneficial for organizations when they need to execute tasks quickly and efficiently. The trust and the established informal ways of working ensure that projects can be delivered with a minimum of fuss and a maximum of shared understanding.

On the other hand, "brokerage" is what's required when leaders and their organizations need to access new ideas, fresh resources and strategic partners. Social networks that are characterized by brokerage are only loosely tied together and may not necessarily share the same values.

This taxonomy leads to two distinctive forms of social capital:

- Bonding capital: this specifically refers to the quality of relationship between people of the same values and social norms: colleagues in well-established teams, close friends and family.
- Bridging Capital: this brings together people who are only loosely connected, who may share similar values but different goals, or vice versa.

Professor Burt goes to great pains to point out that these forms of social capital are distinctive, but are not mutually exclusive. In fact, healthy social networks need both.

Both forms of social capital are important for healthy, sustainable networks. They also have different characteristics: for example, the sum total of "bridging capital" is likely to diminish at a much faster rate than "bonding" capital. Burt, a canny and distinctive researcher, took a considered look at bridging capital in the social networks of bankers. He found that nine out of ten bridging relationships would disappear over the course of one year, despite the fact that they are associated with higher pay levels. There are various possible explanations for this: "bridging" social capital is inherently fragile, being the result of the early stages of any relationships; bridging capital is entirely functional, that is, the relationships are only useful as long as they deliver an obvious result; the individuals may be typical "entrepreneurial leaders" whose focus in relationships is on the short term; or a combination of all three reasons. Whatever the explanation, bridging is clearly not enough in terms of social capital development. Bonding and bridging, as we will see, are equally important in the sustainable value of networks. Both facets of social capital are important for another important and fundamental reason: the value of diversity. Diversity brings richness and freshness to the quality of our relationships. Too often, the ease of the familiar and the similar overrides the possible comfort (and benefits) of strangers. But before we occupy ourselves with the potential downsides, let's look at the benefits of social capital.

THE BENEFITS OF SOCIAL CAPITAL

The specific benefits of social capital can occur at all three levels of social interaction: societal; organizational and individual. Societal benefits may include economic, criminological and educational improvements. For example, academic results show distinct improvements when parents and schools work together.

However, since trends at this macrolevel are not the remit of this book, we will focus on a review of payback for the organization and the individual.

Organizational payback

An organization is an important unit of social capital. In a sense, Putnam's definition referred to earlier has the most transparent application to the understanding and management of social capital. How? At its most basic level, an organization exists in order to ensure the most effective and cost efficient way of achieving its core purpose, irrespective of whether that may be a charity or a merchant bank. As long ago as the 1930's, writers about the existence of organizations recognized that people working together in the joint pursuit of common goals and ambitions could be the least expensive way of achieving those goals. And in particular, researchers in this area have argued that the critical constituent running through the veins of healthy and productive organizations is trust. Organizations that are characterized by trusting relationships both across departments and through layers of hierarchy and status, benefit through the reduction of transaction costs (that is, unnecessary bureaucracy, procedures and paperwork).

A classic example of the triumph of trust over bureaucracy can be seen in Coleman's study of diamond traders. Coleman studied how wholesale diamond traders in the New York diamond market made their money with a marked lack of legal documentation and contractual rubric. He found that this commercial community benefited from a high level of mutual understanding and trust. Incredibly to those on the outside, traders frequently handed over large bags of diamonds to each other without any written contractual arrangements. Their trust-based activity significantly reduced costs involved in dealing with each other and enabled traders to pursue more deals, more often, making more money.

There are innumerable pieces of research that have now been completed which demonstrate the link between high levels of social capital in the work place and positive outcomes for the organization. Many of these have shown that people-focused and trust-based management styles increase morale and productivity. Not only does this approach reap rewards in the short term, but also, as Collins and Porras argue in their book *Built to Last*,[9] ensures that organizations can develop a successful recipe for enduring, long-term success.

A colorful example of the importance of social capital within the complexities of a global organization that works across cultural boundaries on a daily basis was related to us recently by a client, and now a friend, who was then President of a video games company in Europe.

He set the scene:

[T]he excitement and tension was almost tangible in my part of the organization as the launch of a major new generation of our product was imminent. Days before the launch, I received the news from the EU authorities that this particular new device would be classified as a Toy, and that consequently the supplied earphones would have to be changed since the permissible sound pressure level on the specification was too high for children (children's eardrums are more susceptible to damage from high volume than adults').

I was visiting the Chairman in Tokyo when the news reached me and so I spoke directly with him and gently pointed out that perhaps the best solution was to remove the earphones and sell these separately with the appropriate warnings.

Upon hearing this news and realizing the implications (that he could not announce the European version release date at a major upcoming conference in Los Angeles), the Chairman responded in combative style:

"Who says it is a Toy? This is a sophisticated device, it is not a Toy, the earphones stay in, they are an integral part of the device. Change nothing. Executive order."

"But The EU Parliament have very strict rules," I replied.

"Then unless you can convince them that it is not a Toy in 3 days, you are fired!"

"Impossible, maybe 9 months at best, to get the law changed," I responded.

"Then fired!" the Chairman came back.

In the evening we all went to a traditional sushi restaurant; the food was of the highest quality and the "Kubota" sake was the best grade. The next morning, the Chairman called me back in to the office and explained to me that he had had an idea overnight. The new device could be sold without the earphones, he explained; and the Company could market the earphones separately for children and for adults and they would sell more.

Also, not Toy, right?

"What a great idea, I said, why did we not think of that before? No it would not be classified as a Toy in this case"

"I think it was the inspiration from the sake last night," the Chairman replied.

"What about the European Parliament? I asked.

"Fire them all!" he replied but you can stay!"

Our friend had known the Chairman for a number of years and knew that he would suggest the same idea, it just needed some "nomification" (*nomimasu*: to drink in Japanese) and some socializing. There is of course a powerful message in this tale. Our friend had spent the past five years getting to know the Chairman and how important it was to have an immediate solution but one where the Chairman would not lose face. By first hinting at an idea and then socializing, the Chairman was able to suggest a solution of his own, not lose face; and everybody was happy.

However, as anyone who has worked in an organization will tell you, the networks and the shared norms of behavior are just two of the ingredients necessary for effective social capital. There is a third element: sanctions. There has to be consequences in organizations for not behaving in line with either the explicit or implicit expectations of the norms, which shape a social network. In an organizational setting, sanctions may take the form of peer pressure, adverse impact on reward, curtailing career opportunities, clear feedback from line managers, etc. Organizations may articulate trust-based expectations of their people, but frequently fail to reinforce those expectations through effective sanctions. Those sanctions, it should be pointed out, are not always negative; they may be positive and thereby ensure that success is celebrated and encouraged for the future.

Social capital should not be regarded as a property that is exclusively internal to the organization; it may also exist between organizations. Although tricky to put in place, creating strategic alliances between organizations is a great way to develop new products, find new investment and fresh information on markets or other competitors. And there is evidence to suggest that development of inter-firm social capital is worth all the effort and heartache. One recent study in Denmark, United Kingdom and Ireland produced evidence that government-funded programs aimed at fostering more collaboration between small and medium-sized organizations were highly correlated with improved business performance and innovation. And the real proof of this program's effectiveness can be found in the commitment of the organizations involved to invest their own money once the government funding had run out.

Benefits for the individual

It's vital to bear in mind that social capital is not just something that benefits the collective; it has real value for the individual.

In Chapter 2, we briefly mentioned Granovetter's work on the "strength of weak ties" when job hunting. Essentially, this is about developing individual social capital by extending a personal network across separate groups or cliques. This is a great example of "bridging" social capital; and a pure, practical example of "it's not what you know, it's who you know." There is much debate about the proportion of jobs that are filled through informal, personal modes of connection, but some research has suggested that it may be as much as 60 percent of low-wage jobs or as high as 80 percent for jobs in US high-tech organizations. The general trend of such studies is that we ignore the possibilities that may arise through our social capital at our peril.

But man, and entrepreneurs, cannot live through "bridging" alone. Once we have made those connections, we then have to use our own social skills with our new acquaintances to help us achieve the goals we want. Research has shown that entrepreneurs do benefit from the social capital of an extensive network; it also shows that entrepreneurial success relies on building relationships with the people we meet through those connections. The quick message here is we should remember that success is not just about access; it's also about affinity.

There are other benefits, other than access to jobs, which may accrue through individual social capital. Higher wages, better health and getting a better deal from your bank manager have all been identified as benefits of social capital. A key theme here is how you make the most of your social capital and the network in which you find yourself; a topic explored in the next chapter on social networks. We should also note that social capital could be borrowed from others, as well as developed by ourselves.

Kilduff and Tsai are two researchers who know a thing or two about social networks.[10] They studied a $6 billion food company that had a total of 36 different business units: some of these were run by family members that owned the company; while others were run by people from outside the family. Their research had one important finding in this context: individuals in either family or non-family units tended to achieve popularity for themselves by forging a relationship with someone in the other unit that already enjoyed a popular or prestigious status. This is an inverse academic version of "guilty by association." The steady glow of popularity of someone else can augment our own social capital, given the right sort of connection.

Finally, social capital is a potential support mechanism for leaders. Consider our interview in this chapter with Will Hutton. He explicitly mentions the importance of the social capital in his personal networks for his own organizational and thought leadership. They are a source not only of creative ideas, but also personal support and comfort. And he was not alone in making those remarks.

The dark side of social capital

A harsh critic of social capital could point out, not unreasonably, that writers in this area seem to be creating a Coca Cola view of society – one where we "teach the world to sing *together* and live in perfect harmony." Social capital, in this sense, is the quick route to Utopia. It's not true, of course. Putnam devoted a whole chapter to the "dark side" of social capital. We believe that any considered view of this concept has to incorporate a conscious reflection of potential negatives, as well as its possible upsides. To do this, we have to think about the specific nature of the social capital itself, as well as the consequences that might result.

Our first example of adverse social capital takes us to the 1960's, and to the Bay of Pigs misadventure for President Kennedy and his advisers. Faced with the prospect of Castro developing a tight-knit relationship with the communists in Russia and China, Kennedy's administration considered the possibilities of military invasion. Despite the fact that any possible invasion of Cuba would pitch 1,500 marines against 25,000 Castro devotees, a prospect that no one saw as favorable, the Kennedy Administration went ahead with their invasion plans. And what a pig's ear the invasion turned out to be. The explanation for taking a course of action that seemed improbable of success, and ignoring the clear and open concerns of some of Kennedy's cabinet, has been laid at the door of a form of social capital called "Groupthink."

Groupthink occurs when consensus is the driving force of any social unit. Individual and collective experiences are subsumed by a need to agree. There are a number of key features that characterize this unfortunate side of social capital: an illusion of invulnerability; the sanctity of consensus; and the illusion of unanimity. Another chilling example of this lemming-like behavior can be seen in an analysis of the events leading up to the Chernobyl disaster in 1996. The operators within Chernobyl, who are regarded as being those people best placed to have averted this catastrophe, were "consistent with the illusion of invulnerability ... it is likely they rationalised away their worries."[11]

If you believe that you're in the sort of organization that is immune to this sort of collective myopia, consider this example about one of the world's greatest brands, Pepsi. In the early 1980's, Frito-Lay, a Pepsi subsidiary, was the Master of the Snack Food Universe. With their products both profitable and popular, the Frito Lay executives considered themselves immune to the possibility of serious competition. However, as the 80's wore on, Eagle Snack – an upstart brand backed by the marketing might and commercial nous of an Anheuser-Busch – quickly ate into the Frito Lay Market share. The myopic complacency that dominated the Frito Lay organization resulted in the increase of prices ahead of inflation, expanding the numbers of people and pay beyond sensible parameters, while at the same time allowing the quality of the product to fail.

Sometimes it is not the nature of the social capital itself that is an issue, but its crippling consequences. Putnam pointed out that Timothy McVeigh, the Okalahoma City bomber, who executed the worst terrorist atrocity on American soil prior to September 11th, had chatted over possible tactics on an evening of bowling with his fellow right-wingers.

Fukuyama, another American social and political commentator, pointed out that the potential downside of social capital when he observed, "group solidarity in human communities is often purchased at the price of hostility towards out-group members."[12]

In California during 1971, the "in crowd" consisted of surfers and hard-core hippies pursuing fast waves and free love. It was supposed to be a time of liberal lifestyles and open minds; a subculture that made the results of a contemporary social psychological experiment all the more disturbing. Phillip Zimbardo, a psychology professor at Stanford, carried out an experiment sponsored by the Navy to understand sources of conflict between marine guards and their prisoners. It involved college students being randomly allocated to play the role of a guard or the prisoner for two weeks in a simulated prison. However, the "guards" allegedly warmed so quickly to their roles, and became so brutal, that the experiment had to be closed down after only six days. Some of the so-called guards forced prisoners to embrace each other; defecate in buckets and do push-ups as punishment.

This experiment has made Zimbardo famous in psychological circles all around the world. The year 2007 saw him pursue this theme in a book called The *Lucifer Effect: How Good People Turn Evil*, which is a detailed and compelling exploration of how seemingly "normal" people can perpetrate terrible acts.[13] His essential explanation is that personal volition becomes subsumed by the roles and norms of the social system in which they find themselves. He uses this argument to explain the behavior of Ivan Frederick, an army reservist who worked at the Abu Ghraib prison in Iraq. Ivan has been described as a "flag waving, church going husband," a background not obviously conducive to the sort of flagrant acts of human abuse that landed him an eight-year jail sentence. The nature of the prevailing social capital within the US military during this period, argues Zimbardo, led to an act that is only partly attributable to free will.

Our final focus on the less appealing sides of social capital describes perhaps the most obvious potential for damaging consequences: exclusion and elitism. Let's look at exclusion first. It is true to say that many organizations build effective social capital that delivers all of the benefits we have described. Over time, though, the dynamic and fluid nature of those social connections ossifies into a stultified, suffocating organizational climate that continues to bond and forgets to bridge. The consequences? Organizations become out of touch with the markets in which they operate, it becomes staffed with people who hold similar views and have had similar experiences. There are formal studies that have demonstrated a trend for certain entrepreneurial firms to have an optimal level of bonding, after which there becomes an inverse relationship between bonding and organizational success.

Simply, the organization and its people become insulated from the outside world.

Elitism is another potential consequence of social capital. Indeed, for Bourdieu this was the main focus of his studies and thinking. It certainly brings to the fore the importance of power and resources in relation to social capital. In this sense, to really understand the social capital of an organization or its leaders, we have to consider the content and nature of that social capital. Halpern, in his accessible introduction to *Social Capital*, makes the following case:

> Imagine if you compare your social network with that of a billionaire ... the numerical size of your network may not be any different to that of Bill Gates. Indeed your network might have more bridging capital than theirs ... but if we look at the resources the billionaire's network provides access to compared to our own ... we would see a world of difference.[14]

SOCIAL CAPITAL AND ITS IMPLICATIONS FOR LEADERS

In terms of the two core types of social capital development, that is, bridging and bonding, it is relatively easy to see trends in leadership style depending on where individuals prefer to invest their time and energy. From the diagram below (Figure 3.1), this offers the opportunity

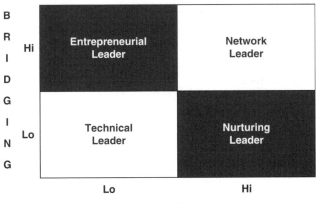

FIGURE 3.1 **The social capital of leadership**

to create a simple typology for leadership style and their pattern of social capital.

We have outlined below some of the dominant features of these different forms of leadership. We will also revisit this framework later in the book to suggest how self-awareness and carefully chosen techniques can help leaders to develop and improve social capital for themselves and their organizations.

The Entrepreneurial Leader

Entrepreneurial leaders exist in a truly borderless world. When they need to get something done, they either already know the right people who can help or will find those people through whatever means is necessary. These leaders are characterized by constantly forming new relationships with people, and by the ability to form those connections quickly. Don't think of this sort of leader in stereotypical terms: they are just as likely to be in your HR or Finance department, as they are in your sales force or your business unit. You'll be able to recognize them by the breadth of their relationships across the organization. They're not likely to just connect people: equally high on their agenda will be bringing together different ideas to create new views on old problems.

The challenge for Entrepreneurial Leaders is that they are driven by bridging and forget to bond. They move on too quickly to the next challenge and the next set of relationships. This means that they may fail to really deliver the potential created by the unique collation of talents and styles of people within their highly diverse networks. The same is true for the ideas: they may move onto the next exciting notion before developing their current conceptual toy to a really satisfactory conclusion.

The Technical Leader

Technical Leaders are turned on by the intrinsic subject matter of their role. At their worst, they don't bridge and don't bond, leaving their ideas and experience locked inside their heads, hidden from the day-to-day world. They are often undervalued because people ignore or misunderstand their actions, and are completely oblivious to their ideas. They may become politically isolated and detached from the real challenges facing an organization. However, organizations ignore these people at their peril. At their best, these leaders can be a constant source of innovation. They may not be the most outwardly entertaining person at the office party, but they may be the most interesting – if you can get them talking. In maps of specific types of social networks, for example, those that try to describe whom people approach for political advice within an organization, the Technical Leader may be found on the fringes. In contrast, for a network that describes whom people seek out for innovative ideas and solutions, these leaders may turn out to be an important hub of activity.

The Nurturing Leader

Leaders who fall into this category are typically highly supportive, encouraging and protective of their people. They are loyal to those around them and actively seek to develop and nurture those people that fall into their network. Their social connections, though, are likely to be highly selective and remain constant over long periods of time. Development of relationships may tend to be reactive and ad hoc rather than proactive and directed. These relationships are likely to be trust-based, but you may have to work hard for that trust in the first place. They create tightly-knit units within organizations – teams with intense loyalty and commitment to each other. The downside with this form of leadership is that those teams are likely to become "cliques" and may become too static in terms of skills and experience composition. For these leaders, it's sometimes a short, sharp step from team commitment and esprit de corps to jobs for the boys and institutional nepotism.

The Network Leader

This form of leader lives in the best of all possible worlds; they bridge and they bond. They exhibit a balanced form of leadership that mixes the old with the new; combine radical approaches with received wisdom; and develop both breadth and depth of relationships. According to our research, network leaders tend to be confident, and increasingly they appear to be women. These attributes enable a leader to be flexible in both their thinking and their behavior, and are likely to be effective across a variety of organizational settings.

Network leaders may not be the universal panacea for organizations. In certain contexts, their typically measured approach may be a little undercharged to deliver change in circumstances where instant and major impact is required. Nevertheless, their dynamic brand of creative connecting and borderless bonding offers much to organizations that want to build a sense of commitment to each other and a set of common goals, regardless of geography, culture, position or capability.

Network Leadership – A case study.

Mott MacDonald is a £900 million business that spans 120 countries with 14,500 staff working in all sectors from transport, energy, buildings, water and the environment to health and education, industry and communications. The breadth of skills of its professional staff, its range of services and its global reach makes it one of the world's top players in delivering management, engineering and development consultancy solutions. An area of significant business growth for Mott MacDonald is Africa where they have a presence in 34 countries, working in sectors ranging from transport, health and education to buildings, stadia, communication and energy. In South Africa alone they now have over 300 staff. Mott MacDonald plays a significant role in the growing development of Africa through the engagement of their health and education experts with worldwide aid organizations as well as with local agencies.

We first met Howard Bate when he was undertaking a senior leadership development program at a European Business School. From the outset it was clear that his role does not fit into any neat organizational box. Howard Bate is MD of Mott MacDonald South Africa and also Regional Director for Africa.

The complexity of simultaneously delivering these two leadership roles became apparent when Howard was asked to sketch his place in the organization chart. Instead of the traditional diagram of horizontal and vertical reporting lines, his rapidly drawn picture immediately

---

included multiple diagonal lines and arrows that crossed and inter-linked – representing his multiple accountabilities and responsibilities. His dialogue as he was sketching went like this:

"As MD of South Africa, my key links are to the Group Business Development Director, the Head of the Transport Division (because our major contracts are within that area just now), the Project Director for that project, and the key contact within Transnet (a major customer)."

That was just one set of radiating lines in his organization chart. Overlaying the equivalents for his Regional Director role immediately added another layer of complexity representing a series of connections that extend his reach even further outside of Mott MacDonald – to Government, Health, Education and Aid organizations. And it is these that he emphasized the most when talking about the opportunities and challenges that Motts faces within Africa.

"The reason we are such a strongly emerging player in Africa is because the opportunities – the projects – are so multifaceted. The infrastructure that we are helping to develop needs to be coherent and joined up across multiple disciplines, professions and functions. We are in a unique position to deliver this – but only if we can com-municate and convince in an equally coherent and joined up way. That is my job basically. To connect the outstanding specialists and project teams that we have, with the clients and their needs. I love doing this."

Asked about what strengths Howard feels that he brings to his role – he answered unequivocally:

"My strengths have always been in business development through rela-tionships. I seem to be able to open doors where others are less successful. They see the bidding process as just that . . . a bidding **process** – rather than starting with a relationship. Although they target individuals – they do not always appreciate that you need to get to know them, and they need to get to know you. Essentially – I need them to really appre-ciate that we are not operating unethically – that we do not take backhanders – that is a real issue in Africa – and makes the difference when looking to win the most substantial and sustainable contracts. You can only do that through personal, face-to-face contact. You have to communicate your personal involvement, commitment and integ-rity. People buy people at the beginning, as well as at the end of the day. Not an elegantly worded bid."

Returning to the web-like drawing of his organizational communication and reporting lines, Howard paused to reflect upon how this helps him to achieve his ambitious growth targets:

"Importantly, it has evolved in recognition that the relationship with the client is primary. We need strong and clear communication internally too – of course – but if that constrains the speed and quality of the client relationship, then we lose the client and the business. I guess that's why it can be difficult to draw and to describe my position in the organization sometimes – once you get beyond job title it becomes an organic structure. Not a structural chart in an electronic or paper document. It makes sense to me and those within it – but it can seem rather slippery if you are looking at it from outside."

Howard became particularly interested in our notion of Network Leadership as we described the concepts of Bridging and Bonding.

"Even without your diagram I would spontaneously have described myself as an entrepreneur. My career path has always taken me into roles with a high degree of marketing and business development responsibility." (Howard has spent time on secondment to McKinsey & Co; founded a project management and controls service company in Spain and set up his own consultancy offering business solutions to the Hong Kong Government). "When setting up or developing companies, I am acutely aware of the make or break nature of relationships. Initially this is all about making the initial connections "Bridging" as you have just described it, into new client groups and markets. You have to devote time "out there" to meet as wide a range of people as possible. Only a small proportion will ultimately pay off as a client – in fact initially almost none will – but they just may lead to someone who will lead to someone. … At that ratio you have to have a continuous pipeline of relationships that you are exploring and nurturing."

We next asked Howard how he decides which relationships to devote time to, he replied,

"[N]ow that's a really intriguing one. Although I've implied the need for quantity, especially when moving into new markets, I find myself instinctively "interviewing" new contacts – trying to identify the likely nature and value of the relationship over time. For example, does this person have the potential to impact my P&L? Can they help me with strategy? What can I offer them as well as what can they offer me? How reciprocal or mutually beneficial might this relationship be over time? And importantly, even if none of these immediately apply, might they be a useful contact for someone else in my network? Because of my role and my contacts within South Africa and Motts, I attract a lot of proactive networking from others. That gives me the luxury of choice as to which ones I prioritize, but also a lot of potential "noise" and distraction if I am not sufficiently disciplined. Often the connection that will be most beneficial to the business is the one that I need to pursue – the one that may not pursue me."

"What your matrix does bring into sharp focus for me though is the need for what you call "Bonding" as well as Bridging. This is something that I have had to more consciously work on in my MD role for South Africa. I am not just the business developer, but also the leader of over 300 people. They quite rightly need and demand my time and presence – to provide vision, direction, pace and reassurance. I can't do that if I am always on a plane to another part of the continent. Finding enough thinking time has been a key leadership challenge for me over the past year. It has taken me 12 months to draw together a really competent management team. In the past they have not been good at managing their staff and I have had to spend a lot of time coaching and developing my managers so that they can become more effective and increasingly autonomous in managing their teams. Many of these individuals are technically brilliant. They have fantastic brains and know their technical stuff better than anyone else in the area. But we need managers – leaders in fact – as our presence and delivery in Africa has grown rapidly. Developing their people skills has been key – and difficult. But I now feel more able to get that balance between connecting with new customers and markets, and providing my team with a sense of clarity and support. Personally – when I am there, and through my management team when I am not. That "Bonding" certainly needs to happen between me and my team, and indeed within my team, but also, as my relationships with my new found connections and relationships deepen and grow – I also need to strengthen those relationships into lasting, trust-based friendships. That's where I came in – developing levels of trust and respect both internally and externally that ultimately make the difference for me as a leader, and for Motts in its competitive market place. Looking again at your model then, I would say that I most naturally fall into the Entrepreneurial Leader quadrant, but that, as a result of my growing people leadership role and the complexity of our African business – I am now simultaneously spending time and energy on the complementary and crucial elements of "bonding" that pull me into that Network Leadership quadrant."

So let's not be carried away by a four-box model. Some people may not collapse neatly into one of these four categories. Shifting contexts may bring about shifting behaviors. The purpose of this model is to develop self-awareness and understanding in order to maximize the leadership opportunities to develop the right sort of social capital. But even when we understand our leadership preferences and the possible patterns of interactions, how do we confirm that understanding, whether conscious or intuitive? Relationships are ultimately intangible and invisible. How do we make the invisible, visible?

4

MAKING THE INVISIBLE VISIBLE

INTRODUCTION

Michael Frayn, novelist, playwright and columnist, perhaps most famous for his plays, *Copenhagen* and *Noises Off*, articulated a canny insight about our perception of the universe. In his book, *The Human Touch*, he notes that when we look up at the night sky, beyond our luminous moon and deep into the Milky Way, we only see "that calm seems certainly safe tonight."[1] In other words, we perceive our galaxy as an ocean of stillness, a place where nothing much seems to happen because it is invisible to our naïve eye. Frayn makes the point that, in reality, we are barreling around the Sun, and the Sun around the galaxy at incredible speeds; and that aside from our speedy galactic travels, the universe is a maelstrom of unseen explosions and collisions. It is only thanks to the science and technology of astronomy that we can make the invisible hustle and bustle of space *visible*, so that we can wonder at the universe and ponder our place within it.

The myriad of social connections that link people to each other are no different to the invisible cosmos. We cannot see these ties of affinity and antipathy, but they exist with all the complexity, commotion and dynamism of space. Chapter 2 described how networks generally are a ubiquitous feature of the twenty-first century life; the purpose of this chapter is to describe how the nascent discipline of social network analysis enables us, by making the invisible visible, to consciously consider our social worlds and to proactively shape our participation within them.

Dr Bruce Cronin, Director of the Centre for Economic Analysis at the Greenwich Business School, and a keen but critical network analyst, regards this area to be not unlike the early days of astronomy: the technology is crude and the theory is lacking, but there can be no doubt that the results so far have generated a mass of "interesting and exciting data that illuminate our social world." The astronomy analogy is no coincidence: Bruce's lecture halls and offices are a short walk from the famous Greenwich observatory. Established in 1675 by Charles II, the observatory had been built to improve navigation through astronomy so that sailors would be able to pinpoint their location, particularly when out of land's sight. Social network analysis promises us the capability to navigate the seas of social connections with equal confidence.

However, in the view of experts such as Dr Cronin, the field is still fraught with potential misunderstanding and misconceptions; when confronted with network maps, people are seduced into believing that the map represents reality rather than a particular version of that reality. To demonstrate to people the interpretive nature of that map, the authors run a specific exercise during workshops on social capital.

Simply, we divide the audience into two groups – A and B. We tell group A that we are about to give them an example of a network map that is conducive to organizational effectiveness; while for group B, we tell them that we are giving them a network map that hinders organizational success. Neither of the groups sees the other group's map. Of course, we give them a copy of the same network map, an example of which you can see overleaf.

Typically the responses are as follows:

Group A
- Everyone has some route to connect to everyone else.
- Barnes acts as a key broker for all the clusters, speeding up the flow of information and ensuring that it can reach all points in the network.
- Wallis (SE Regional Director) has a strong, direct relationship with Barnes.
- The organization is not limited to top-down, hierarchical forms of communication (e.g., Johnson [Area Manager 3] has direct contact with Wong [non-manager Area 2]).
- Only 2 people have only one direct contact. All the rest have between 2 and 10.

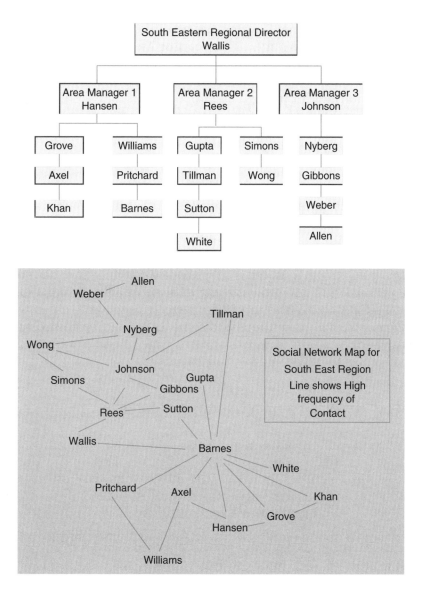

FIGURE 4.1 **Example of network map**

Group B

- Barnes has all the power. If he leaves or becomes disgruntled, he is in a position to fragment the network.

- Wallis (SE Regional Director) has no direct contact with Johnson (his direct line report), or any part of Area 3. Similarly he only connects to Hansen and Area 1 through Barnes.
- Area 1 appears to be very isolated. No direct contact into the other functions except through Barnes.
- Johnson has a very removed path of connection with Allen, one of his reports.

The temptation to reify a world captured in attractive two-dimensional space, with apparent lines of connection ripe with potential meaning, is overwhelming for some people. Our exercise is just a simple but effective technique to remind people of the potential interpretive difficulties with network maps; and to underline the importance of context.

Our goal in this chapter is to provide a succinct overview that enables readers to adopt their own critical perspective, to avoid some of the pitfalls and to use that critical perspective to put to use in their own context. This is not intended to be an exhaustive and comprehensive introduction to network analysis; the subject is too rich and too complex to be covered in a single chapter.

SOCIAL NETWORK ANALYSIS: CORE CONCEPTS

At a recent conference based in a prestigious UK business school, the topic of conversation was how do higher educational institutions engage the private sector more effectively. The audience consisted mostly of vice chancellors and human resource professionals. At the end of the conference, all the participants were asked a single question: what was the "take-away," the one golden nugget of conversation that had made the day worth attending. Frankly, most people scratched their heads and struggled to articulate something concrete. However, one thing had become apparent: the importance of language. Both of these "tribes," divided by a need on the one hand to "educate" and on the other to improve performance, inhabit a different cultural space, and their vocabulary had created the walls that insulated them from each other. This language gap had erected barriers to entry to each others' worlds, which sometimes during the course of this day appeared insurmountable.

On a related theme, one of the mysteries of social capital and social network maps that baffled the authors of this book for some time is this: The world of social networks and social capital offers potentially valuable insights for both organizations and individuals, so why isn't it more popular? In writing this book, and pushing further into the arena, the reason became clear: the language gap. There is a plethora of confusing vocabulary and arcane terminology that, for the average person wanting to extract something useful to put to work in their own organizations, requires an excessive investment of time. As this chapter unfolds, we hope to clarify some of this language in order to make it more accessible to a general audience. This may mean that we omit some of the subtle nuances associated with the specific language. We make no apology. This area is too important for organizations and their leaders to ignore the tools and techniques because they don't appreciate the shades of meaning implicit within some of the specialist language.

Part of the challenge of leaping the language gap is that the social network arena has developed its thinking and its techniques from a number of distinct but frequently overlapping approaches. There are at least "three tribes" of social network investigation worth mentioning in this context. But remember that the goal of this chapter is not to delve into the technical detail of each approach, but to give the general reader a broad sense of the different strands with some of the key insights that may be useful from an organizational perspective.

The three tribes are

- **Sociological – a person-centered approach:** which examines both quantitatively and qualitatively the nature of social relationships.
- **Mathematical – a number-centered approach:** which uses mathematics and modern computer science to examine the *structure* and properties of social networks.
- **Interactionist:** which draws its inspiration and insight from physics, and which considers the interaction between the individual and the social context.

All of these approaches come along with their own conceptual and linguistic baggage, as well as contributing to the evolution of a specific lingua franca for operatives in this field. Consequently, it's worth looking at all three of these techniques not only to clarify concepts and words, but also in order to understand the conceptual *and* practical danger zones that come along with any form of social network analysis.

A sociological approach: The people eaters

The wind-swept streets of Chicago, once the capital of the iron network in the United States (the railroad), has always been a big draw for people interested in observing human behavior. As a hub of activity for finance, industry and culture in the American Midwest, the city affords a glimpse into every possible layer of human society. In the 1920's and 1930's, Chicago was an interesting place to be for understanding how informal networks undermine formal organizational rules and structure. This period of US history is perhaps better known to us as "The Prohibition Era," brought about by the influence of the Temperance movement on US lawmakers, and which resulted in a legal ban on the manufacture and transportation of alcohol. Still, in the words of entrepreneurs the world over: "see a need, fill a need." Rather than the United States becoming a drink-free role model for the world over, a network of crime syndicates sprung up all over the country to create a powerful, profitable black market. Perhaps the most famous exponent of this so-called racketeering was a notorious denizen of Chicago, Al Capone. His underground network of criminal associates, more typically referred to as a crime "syndicate," made pay through their own "moonshine," and other related activities.

During roughly the same period, a man called Elton Mayo conducted perhaps the earliest, formal social network studies in an organizational context.[2] Eschewing the rich possibilities of studying networks with the Chicago gangs of the time, he opted for the far safer option of understanding informal relationships at the Western Electric Company in Chicago between 1924 and 1932. These studies are generally referred to as The Hawthorne Studies.

A latecomer to the world of sociology, it was not until Mayo was forty-six that he turned his focus to applying sociological thinking to management theory. Essentially, Elton Mayo's contribution to organizational theory and practice has been the emphasis on the essential and fundamental social nature of human beings, a need that inevitably manifests itself in a work context. He demonstrated this need during his studies of the Bank Wiring Observation Room at the Hawthorne

Plant of WEC. Although narrow in scope, and not without their critics, these studies demonstrate the power of what we call "social network analysis" and, although completed almost eighty years ago, are relevant today.

Broadly speaking, the studies were established to understand the impact of incentives on people in this particular context. Managers in the wiring room had tried to raise productivity but without success. Executives within the organization were scratching their heads as to why this was the case. They had to create formal structures to enhance efficiency, and introduced incentives that offered a rational stimulus for individuals to operate more productively. Why wasn't their grand plan working?

The Bank Wiring Observation Room consisted of 14 people: nine wirers divided into three subgroups, one supervisor for each of these smaller groups and two inspectors that moved between all three. Careful study of the informal interactions between these groups brought to light the existence of two influential cliques that had a significant impact on the output of the group as a whole. The informal groups created their own informal leaders and a set of implicit rules that actually governed production:

1. You should not deliver too much work; those that did were regarded as "rate busters."
2. Conversely, you should not turn out too little work – an occurrence that led to the term "chisler."
3. You should not tell the supervisor anything that may have a detrimental impact on any of your colleagues.
4. You should refrain from acting officious – being part of the group was critical.

These implicit social rules would have remained unknown and unknowable without a conscious study of these small-scale, social networks.

If that sort of informally organized, industrial resistance appears to be something from yesteryear, consider these thoughts from Peter Scraton, a twenty-first century HR Director with a pedigree in such globally recognized brands as Pepsi and Heinz:

> When you embark on serious change programmes, all of my experience tells me that one should never underestimate the power of informal relationships to subvert effective change.

The results of Mayo are as relevant today as they were in the heyday of prohibition.

A very different study, conducted far from the claustrophobic conditions of the Bank Wiring Room in 1920's Chicago, and one that is of a more social anthropological tradition, is Kapferer's analysis of labor unrest in Zambia during the early 1970's.[3] Kapferer, based at the world-recognized school of Social Anthropology at Manchester University, went to Zambia during a period of great social upheaval. One of the most striking aspects of this study from a practical perspective is that it focused on how deliberate, intentional changes in social relationships by specific actors led to industrial action by workers in a garment factory. Critically, Kapferer's work actually predicted destabilization of the business based on those changes in social dynamics.

An important factor in Kapferer's study in adding real, pragmatic value is that it consisted of two phases conducted over an eight-month period. This gave him some longitudinal data to understand the impact of changes over a significant time period. During phase one, he noted that senior, more militant workers in the factory were unable to secure wage and work improvements, despite attempting to organize several walkouts. Seven months later, these same men were able to incite a strike that resulted in the desired improvements. Kapferer attributed the result to a significant shift in what network analysts call, "centralization." Centralization is an important concept in social networks and refers to the extent that a specific network is centralized around one, or a few, social actors. Networks with low levels of centralization tend to be loosely affiliated and are unlikely to be characterized by co-ordinated activity. Conversely, up to a certain point, networks with high centralization demonstrate high levels of cohesion with the potential for group action. Phase one of the study demonstrated a low centralization score, indicating the lack of concerted leadership necessary to encourage collective action. In contrast, phase two of the project showed a marked increase in centralization, a result of *more people being linked into a common set of interactional relationships.* As a result, these militant workers were able to exert significantly more influence and bring about strike action in support for a £1 wage increase.

There are two important aspects of this study that we should remember when studying social networks. Firstly, context is critical. Kapferer's work combined network detail with real understanding of the cultural, political and social context. He knew who the players were in the network, their motivations and their aspirations. This helped him to ask the right questions of the data and not to draw conclusions from a specific network map. If anything, it only posed more questions for him. Secondly, the value of the work is not the network at any point in time, but the dynamics of the network as it evolved over a specific period of time. In this sense, the network maps are "photographs" of a frozen moment in the evolution of social relationships. However, Kapferer produced a "moving picture" of those relationships which offered insight into the nature of networks (the relevance of centralization) and how it may impact on the wider organizational structure.

A mathematical approach: The number crunchers

In Chapter 2, we talked about the "small world phenomenon": the pervasive finding that we are connected to each other by fewer intermediaries (or nodes) than we might have anticipated. This is a critical feature of the mathematical approach to networks. An analytical, mathematical approach has delivered the quantitative evidence that small worlds aren't just a feature of social networks, but extend way and beyond to all sorts of other forms of networks such as power grids and neural networks. The rigor and replication afforded through the use of various mathematical tools are important to demonstrate the integrity of this phenomenon. The results of psychological experiments conducted by people like Stanley Milgram have been scrutinized and criticized many times over: for a particularly rough treatment, have a look at Parker's 1972 article in *Granta*'s "Shrinks."[4]

Mathematical techniques and computer software have brought about new and imaginative uses for the small world effect. For example, the authors of this book have a mutual friend who makes the most out of the small world phenomenon. There exists in the Internet world a software program called The Oracle of Elvis. Hosted by the University of Virginia, it enables you to discover the number of steps between any actor and Elvis Presley.[5] An Elvis "number" indicates the degree of separation from Elvis. For example, that old ham of horror Vincent Price appeared in a film called *Trouble with Girls* with Elvis. He therefore receives an Elvis number of (1). Bob Hope, on the other hand, has an Elvis number of (2): he never appeared in a film with Elvis, but appeared in a film with Vincent Price, who did. Our aforementioned friend is an ex-actor (and no offence – he knows who he is – but is not really known in a theatrical sense outside of a very tight dramatic circle in the East End of London) but has an Elvis number of (3). A fact that he communicates to anyone prepared to listen, and quite a few that are not! The fact that it is only a few short steps between his short-lived acting career and the King of Rock and Roll is a great illustration of the small world phenomenon.

A different view of small world episodes is what Malcolm Gladwell in a *New Yorker* article in 2008 describes as the "phenomenon of simultaneous discovery."[6] Whereas our commonsense view of the world tends to see inventions and discoveries as being the product of the imaginative endeavors of a single individual; the history of science tells us that in fact individuals working on the same scientific challenge *independently*, and often ignorant of each others' efforts, often converge on the same solution at roughly the same time.

In Gladwell's counter-intuitive article, he points out that one of the most historic examples is the simultaneous invention of calculus by Leibniz and Newton in the seventeenth century. As always in these situations, there was the usual brouhaha focused on which of the two men should be attributed with being the lone genius and the person who had come to these ideas first. Gladwell argues that when this occurred, it was because "calculus was in the air." What Gladwell meant by this is that both men shared the intellectual trails left by other scientific forerunners. Although it seemed from their own vantage point that they each enjoyed a lone island of independent discovery; in reality they inhabited the same intellectual archipelago surrounded by a common ocean of earlier thoughts and discoveries by their predecessors.

A similar event occurred in the world of networks in a few short months between 2002 and 2003. Two of the most significant contributors to this field from a mathematical perspective, Albert-Laszlo Barabasi and Duncan J. Watts, published independently, and within a few months of each other, two books that aimed at bringing the science of networks to a wider audience.[7, 8] Both books share lots of common ideas and themes: six degrees of separation, Stanley Milgram, graph theory and more. Interestingly, even in the small world of social networks, there are some important differences, too. Where their thoughts do converge is on the topic of a man who laid down some of the key principles of a central area in this mathematical approach to network science: Paul Erdos. Erdos was a somewhat eccentric, itinerant, Hungarian mathematician who is renowned for the incredible number of papers he published during his lifetime (approximately

1500). Aside from his prodigious mathematical ability, he was also recognized as someone with an open, intellectual spirit who would collaborate with anyone, if the problem were of sufficient interest and his collaborators equipped with enough mental agility. In total, over the course of his lifetime, he had 507 co-authors, some of whom then went on to collaborate with each other. Paul Erdos was a living, breathing social network. Just like the "Elvis numbers" mentioned earlier, mathematicians talk about "Erdos Numbers," which measure the collaborative distance between the author of any mathematical paper and the great man himself.[9] To see an example of the collaborative network of Paul Erdos visit www.orgnet.com/Erdos.html

Erdos, in partnership with Albert Renyi, developed the theory of random graphs. However, as Watts points out in his book *Six Degrees*, "random graph theory is not for the faint hearted" being a particularly inaccessible branch of science. Here are some essentials to keep us on track. A graph is a formal, mathematical term for describing the pattern of connections we see in networks. At its most fundamental, a graph is a set of points or nodes connected by lines or edges. A network is exactly that, where the "nodes" that we're talking about in this context are actually people, and the lines of connection, relationships. For those with a mathematical inclination, random graph theory promises to deliver a formal, mathematical basis for the properties and behaviors of networks.

Both Watts and Barabasi explain the work of Erdos and Renyi through straightforward analogies in order to demonstrate a fundamental finding in network science (Watts uses the idea of buttons thrown on the floor and then randomly connected by string; while Barabasi talks of random people at a party who are all unknown to each other). When there are few connections between independent nodes (buttons/people) in any network (or graph), unsurprisingly, nothing interesting happens because nothing is really connected to anything else. However, when we create a situation, in which each node has on average at least one connection to one other node, then the network goes through a remarkable change – it becomes highly interconnected and enables a plethora of network phenomena, depending on the context: faster communication, the diffusion of innovations, the rapid spread of disease. *It is at this point of optimal connection that the small world phenomena begin to occur.* What's really interesting about this non-mathematically is that it is easy to assume that to develop that level of connectivity, most nodes need lots of connections. This clearly isn't the case.

But, as both Watts and Barabasi argue, the perfect world of random graphs envisaged by Erdos and Renyi is a long way from the messy world of real networks, particularly where people are concerned. However, this approach does offer a couple of interesting angles that are worth considering from a practical perspective: Firstly, and in contrast to the Kapferer study earlier in the chapter, networks may not always need the influence of co-ordinating actors to deliver some form of value for an organization. In fact, you could imagine a network where high levels of centralization around a few people (or nodes) within a network would actually undermine its usefulness in certain situations.

The need for diversity for healthy networks is given a fresh insight from this simple mathematical observation. We might assume that in order to introduce the requisite richness of difference, individuals within that network need a large number of contacts to which they are connected. This may not be the case. If each member of that network includes only one other unique connection, then the network itself should benefit. However, we should recall Burt's work on brokerage and closure in Chapter 3. It's not sufficient to find the new contact and introduce to the existing network (brokerage), we also have to embed that person in the network in order to derive real value (closure).

Our practical experience is consistent with this conclusion. Recently, the authors took a group of engineers that had worked together closely over a number of years. Their network was insular at best. We encouraged each engineer, having identified their business and individual goals over the ensuing twenty-four months, to identify one new person who existed outside that network, either within the organization or outside, that might be able to support the delivery of those goals. Individually, the engineers were great at doing this, being proactive and creative in their approach. However, the insularity of the network created real barriers to new thoughts and approaches being adopted. Simply put, the hard work came not at the point of brokerage, but at closure – integrating those ideas into the thoughts and practices of the team as a whole. Critically, though, the exercise did demonstrate the value of the original mathematical principle.

This is an important point when considering building innovation networks in organizations. When encouraging executives to develop their own networks, more introverted individuals are likely to imagine a torturous process whereby they are expected to put themselves through the difficult and artificial process of developing and maintaining relationships with lots of different people with whom they would rather not. In workshops run by the authors, the very word "networking" for some people conjures up horrendous images of corporate-ladder-climbing-clones passing out random business cards during conferences in the hope of making some sort of useful connection with people. Conversely, the real extroverts, at the mere mention of social activity, are already heading toward the door with a playful glint in their eye at the notion that talking to new people might be considered a legitimate working activity. Erdos and Renyi's work on random graph theory suggests that both the introverts and the extroverts can relax a little. As Elvis himself put it, possibly great social networks involve "a little less conversation" than we imagine.

The work by Watts, Barabasi and scientists of a similar ilk has provided a mathematical foundation for the qualitative observations of sociologists and psychologists. The recurrent theme of the small world phenomenon is not just anecdotal; the finding also has a mathematical basis. This fact may be more important to some readers than others: its inclusion in a book on leadership is based on the desire to offer different but converging lines of evidence for taking properties of networks seriously. We want leaders to investigate and understand networks more comprehensively in order to shape and inform their strategic decisions and their leadership behaviors.

But let's not get carried away. Watts warns us at the end of his book that "claiming everything is a small world network ... can mislead one to think that the same characteristics are relevant to every problem." This branch of network science is still in its infancy: there may be new forms of network and new insights around network functionality that become important to understand for organizations and their leaders.

The interactionist perspective

Although the techniques described earlier in the chapter have made the invisible world of social connections visible to the interested observer, the personality and the behaviors of the individuals at the heart of the networks remain indiscernible.

At a recent, global get-together of networking experts and enthusiasts, an interesting episode occurred during one of the more "academic" sessions. When asked by a member of the audience whether or not the speaker had applied "network analytics" to his essentially historical, anthropological data the speaker replied, haltingly: "No. Life has always seemed too short to me to take that approach." This off-the-cuff, ironic remark, in a session otherwise characterized by a lack of humor, struck the collective funny bone of the audience. There was a raucous burst of laughter and a spontaneous round of applause. We'd seen nothing like this in any previous sessions. It was an episode that continued to linger and intrigue us at the end of the day. This ironic, implicit and perhaps unintended criticism of this small world of network studies struck a real chord with everyone. The audience's reaction seemed to ask the question: where are the people, the human beings, in the field of social networks? For a science that should have some soul, researchers in the field seemed to be irrevocably immersed in a rather mechanistic approach. In fact, Professor Burt, who developed the brokerage and closure concepts, had this to say about a purely mathematical approach: "beware the machine men!"

To reconcile the person and the social is a real challenge for psychology and sociology generally, not just the field of leadership specifically. Some of the more experienced authors in this sector have said that "to speak of personality and social structure in the same breath is as close as one can get to heresy." This should not come as a surprise to anyone. The authors of this book have worked in the fields of both clinical and organizational psychology; and it has taken a long time for the two subdisciplines of psychology to draw on mutual insights and experience in order to solve practical problems. When it's a question of drawing together insights from what seem to be, on the surface at least, very different disciplines, the intellectual friction increases exponentially to the point it may seem impossible or insane to try to bridge what Burt would describe as a "structural hole."

As a personal example, the authors recently presented to a group of academics from a leading business school in the United Kingdom. One clique of the audience represented a sociological view of the world; while a second clique argued their case from a psychological point of view. Normally, these people wouldn't be caught breathing the same air as each other. However, today a common enemy united them: the idea that sociology and psychology should come together to provide a more unified perspective on leadership. As the proponents of that idea, we received a fair degree of scorn and venom. On reflection over a glass of wine later that evening, the behavior seemed to emphasize the importance of adopting an interactionist approach to leadership: a view where we could talk sensibly about the leader in context, drawing insight and guidance from the network science of sociology as well as psychological data and theory.

Duncan Watts is a one-time physicist-turned-sociology professor. In his terrific book about social networks called *Six Degrees*, he states, "Physicists, it turns out, are almost perfectly suited to invading other people's disciplines … physicists see themselves as Lords of the Academic Jungle." Although the statement does seem to suffer from an unhealthy dose of scientific hubris, as non-physicists there is some truth to what Watts is saying. Theoretical physicists in particular carve a path against the grain of intuition. Their observations about the laws of nature shouldn't be overlooked when coming to grips with the principles of human nature. In Chapter 1, we quoted and paraphrased the overlord of physics, Albert Einstein, who said "Physical objects exist not in space, but these objects are spatially extended (as fields)." Now what physicists would term "classic field theory" refers to how forces such as electromagnetism and gravity interact with physical objects in a continuous manner. This concept of fields has been extended by psychologists to elucidate how the environment may impact on the choices and behaviors of the individual.

Kurt Lewin, regarded by some as the Father of modern social psychology, was a contemporary of Einstein and, unsurprisingly, was influenced by Einstein's view of the universe. Lewin's essential perspective on people and how they behave was that "human behaviour is a function of both the person and the environment."[10] Not rocket science, as they say, but so easily forgotten when it comes to trying to understand leaders and their behavior. To be more exact, Kurt defined his "field" as "the totality of co-existing facts which are conceived as mutually interdependent." Individual behavior changes as we perceive, interpret and act upon those facts. Our notion is a twist on that definition. We would regard the "field" as being "the totality of social relationships in which we exist." Our behavior changes as we perceive, interpret and act upon those relationships and the interconnections between them. To be blunt, the research in this area is thin on the ground. Where it exists, the methods and the conclusions often pose more questions than they answer.

There are sound reasons for this, aside from the normal chasm that separates different academic disciplines. If every conceptual journey begins with a single step, where does someone begin with this? Do you start with thinking about the person or the social context? To begin with, we need to be clear about what we mean by "person" or "personality." What approach do we use to describe that personality? Some researchers use a trait-based approach, which is a bottom-up methodology that crunches all possible verbal descriptors of personality and produces a succinct taxonomy. (By the way, it's an incredible coincidence that publishers of these sorts of profiles find that the sum total of human personality fits neatly into A4 size documentation.) An alternative approach is to take a "top-down" view and begin with a major theory about personality types and then construct a more detailed typology on the basis of that theory. The MBTI® questionnaire, used all over the world and based on Jungian psychology, is an example of this approach.[11] To take a completely different approach, some psychologists ignore descriptors of personality and stick with the purely behavioral.

Conversely, if you opt to start with the social context, how do you make sense of that typically complex social space? You can opt to focus on the structure of the networks, and analyze individuals who feature more or less prominently in different areas of a social network. Alternatively, we know that the development of healthy networks can be segmented into brokerage and closure – does this framework become the starting point?

Burt and his colleagues at the Chicago business school have conducted one interesting foray into an interactive approach.[12] They examined the networks of a group of MBA students. They asked every student to complete a psychological profile and then went in search of some interesting "connections." Of course, as the researchers point out, the results can't really speak to causality, that is, does the personality shape the network or does the network shape the personality? What it does achieve is to highlight which psychological patterns are prevalent, and to some extent successful, within a specific sort of network. In this particular study, they found that people with loosely connected networks with ties that leap across a number of structural holes are more likely to describe their personality in broad terms as being that of an "entrepreneurial outsider," whereas individuals with an essentially tight-knit network regarded themselves as "conforming insiders."

The problem with this work, you might say, is that the observations are based on the otherworldly participants (MBA students) of a business school.

Recognizing this argument, Burt's colleagues went on to develop an index of "entrepreneurial personality" and to explore the personality and the networks of several hundred corporate employees of a financial organizational. The participants were drawn from a diverse cross-section of roles, and here the results become very interesting.

Firstly, there is an interesting distinction between individuals who are lower in the corporate hierarchy and more senior individuals. For the former, there is a strong correlation between a self-reported "entrepreneurial personality" and the sort of loosely connected networks you might expect for that type of character. However, neither the personality profile nor the network structure has been found to be linked with performance for these people. In contrast, for senior managers, there *is* a link between an entrepreneurial network and better performance, but not a link with personality. Confused? Well, the argument goes that for senior managers, regardless of personality type, having a network that glues together people across structural holes is important for good performance. It doesn't matter that you might not see yourself as an "entrepreneurial character"; it's a pre-requisite for getting things done. Roles at the bottom end of the hierarchy are more task focused, and so don't need the same level or sort of social capital. Loosely connected, entrepreneurial networks are therefore more discretionary.

The work is more suggestive than conclusive and it does focus on only one aspect of social capital, that is, brokerage. Of course, there is a different form of social capital that is likely to be useful to leaders, closure, but which may need a different approach and different behaviors. Closure depends on having strong ties with people and is often an important element in the influencing and persuasion of others. Leaders with strong relationships with their people foster loyalty, trust, commitment and respect. Much of the work on leadership has focused on this more obvious and more traditional facet of a leader's role.

To understand the connection between the individual and closure, Professor Beverley Alimo-Metcalfe took a different approach to Burt and his colleagues. Rather than look at the relationship between personality and social capital, Professor Alimo-Metcalfe focused on leadership behaviours.[13] She opted for this route for a number of reasons; not least of which is that behavior is observable and is less susceptible to the conceptual debates of personality-based research. Her work is characterized by a healthy pragmatism and makes a studied avoidance of quixotic traits such as "charisma."

Key to her work is the use of a psychological technique called "360° feedback." This technique entails the elicitation of views from a range of people with whom a leader comes into contact: their staff, peers, customers, the boss and even strategic partners. Data is gathered using a structured framework that requests feedback according to a specific range of behavioral criteria. Those invited to give feedback do so by evaluating behavior against a simple numerical scale and, in some instances, there may be the opportunity to leave some qualitative, free-form feedback during the course of the process. The recipient of the feedback then receives a report which presents the data with the patterns and trends in a variety of ways.

Professor Alimo-Metcalfe's first step in developing her own 360° profiling tool was to avoid falling foul of the hagiography that typifies much leadership development. Rather than asking leaders what makes them effective – with all the danger of self-deluding response bias – she asked the people that had been on the receiving end of their behaviors. Over a period of time she developed a robust set of behavioral "clusters" that time and again seemed essential for leaders if they are to develop strong, loyal ties (with real performance benefits). Her next step was to build a 360-degree questionnaire to capture feedback on these behaviors from different stakeholders, and to create a report that provided the highlights and lowlights of that feedback to the leader in question.

This work provides real insight into some of the core behavioral constituents of closure: for example, demonstrating a genuine interest in someone's development; empowering others to use their initiative; establishing clear goals for the individual and teams. Using this technique to identify clear behaviors that can be observed and evaluated is potentially valuable for leaders. More often than not, it is a huge wake-up call for people to focus less on the task and more on the people aspects of their roles. Of course, in highlighting the behaviors it still falls into the classic informational hole for 360-feedback – it doesn't tell you anything about the nature of the relationship between the leader and the respondents. This "gap" leads to intricate rationalizations from leaders when discussing the less positive aspects of 360-feedback with them. Some of the more common explanations for patterns of poor or indifferent feedback is, "I don't see those people very often" or "I don't think they like me that much," or "we have a very different approach," etc. In a sense, it shouldn't matter because the feedback is a reflection of perception – and that is the reality in which a leader exists. Still, because there is no relationship information, it is an important point to consider. In contrast, Burt's study is rooted in those relationships and provides a clear sense of the social ties that result from a leader's frequency and nature of interaction with other people. But it doesn't tell you anything about behavior.

So when we're talking about "making the invisible, visible," it's a tricky business. From a leadership perspective, we really need to bring to the surface the purpose, frequency and quality of relationships in order to understand the social capital that leaders might have available to them. It's critical to note, however, that social capital isn't homogenous – we could be talking about social capital resulting from brokerage or closure. This means that behaviors will differ in relation to those structural differences in relationship networks. The tools we have to explore social networks and how individuals operate within those networks are not perfect. Social networking techniques tell us something about those relationships, but little about behavior. When psychologists use their tools to take a closer look at behavior, we then lose information about the quality of relationships.

But let's not lose heart. The first telescope at the Royal Observatory was nothing to write home about. In essence it was no more than a 5-ft. brass tube with a glass aperture of 1.5 inches and a magnification of less than x 40. Let's contrast that with the telescopic behemoth floating 350 miles about the Earth – the Hubble Telescope. It has a 2.4 meter mirror and enabled mankind to see further in space and time than ever before. In terms of making the invisible visible, perhaps one of the Hubble's more photogenic successes has been the formation of stars in the Eagle Nebula (see Figure 4.2).

FIGURE 4.2 **Picture of Eagle Nebula**

Source: Stsci.edu 2 November 1995 photo STSCI-PRC95-44a; photo credit Jeff Hester Scowen (Arizona State University) and NASA.

Never before have we been able to see a cosmic spectacle of this degree in the blackness of space. Similarly, technology for mapping social networks will evolve, as will the psychological tools for understanding human cognition and behavior in the midst of social activity. However, in the absence of "Hubble power" for leadership development, perhaps other areas of psychology might offer more insight and illumination

5

THREE CIRCLES OF NETWORK LEADERSHIP

INTRODUCTION

A poet once said, "The whole universe is in a glass of wine."
(Richard Feynman, Nobel prize-winning physicst)[1]

Caltech, or the The California Institute of Technology, is distributed over 124 acres of land in Pasadena, California. With 32 Nobel prizes to its name (for 31 recipients – Linus Pauling won two prizes for chemistry and peace!), Caltech is an institution with a fearsome reputation for intellectual excellence. In the 1960's, roughly about the time that Zimbardo stretched the ethical limits of experimental psychology at Harvard, Richard Feynman was Professor of Theoretical Physics and working furiously on a range of problems at the boundaries of science.

Feynman, who won a Nobel prize for quantum physics, has a reputation for being more than a first rate physicist. He was renowned for his excellent teaching skills, his sense of humour and his fine bongo playing, which you can sample if you follow this link to YouTube: www.youtube.com/watch?v=qWabhnt91Uc. In a sense, he was something of a Renaissance man in that his interests and passions ranged from microbiology to music and art, and he had a personality that always insisted on seeing the whole picture from the macro to the micro. And a glass of wine was no exception to Professor Feynman:

If our small minds, for some convenience, divide this glass of wine, this universe, into parts – physics, biology, geology, astronomy, psychology, and so on – remember that nature does not know it! So let us put it all back together, not forgetting ultimately what it is for. Let it give us one more final pleasure; drink it and forget it all!

His words of warning serve as a useful caveat as we enter our next chapter. So far, we have really looked for clues about leadership and social capital working from the "outside-in," that is, examining the social context and moving to inferences about leaders in terms of their psyche and their behaviors. For the next phase of our story, we want to take a step away from the social and adopt a more individual and more psychological perspective. Firstly, we'll take a look at what contemporary psychologists are telling us about how human beings may have evolved to develop relationships. We'll examine some of the evidence that breaks down human psychological traits and preferences into possible differences between men and women. Then we're going to focus on deconstructing the psychology of leadership specifically and propose three clusters of thinking strategies and behaviors that have emerged from our own investigations (cognitive flexibility, strategic resilience and network excellence). Our three-circle model breaks down further into a range of behaviors and cognitive processes. We believe that these capabilities are likely to be highly useful when trying to leverage social capital for leadership purposes.

But we shouldn't lose sight of the fact that, as Richard Feynman points out, "we need to put it all back together, and not forget what [leadership] is for." And regardless of circumstances and in the face of all challenges, the purpose of leadership is to deliver results. Network leadership, as we've loosely called the combination of behaviors, thoughts and feelings in this chapter, can't deliver those results without the creative combination of all of the constituent elements; and they need to occur in a nuanced way that is sensitive to situation and context. Like a memorable glass of wine, great leadership is at least the sum of its parts. And possibly more.

THE FUTURE IS BRIGHT; THE FUTURE IS FEMALE?

After announcing his engagement to friends and family in 2003, a colleague received an unusual present from a family friend to celebrate the event. The friend was Professor Brian Sykes, a geneticist from Oxford University, and the present was a signed copy of his latest book, entitled: *Adam's Curse: A Future without Men.*[2] Inside there was a small, wry inscription which said, "Congratulations! And don't worry, it won't happen for another 125,000 years!" The essential argument in this provocative book is that the Y chromosome is decaying at the rate of knots, with the continuing loss of hundreds of genes. This inexorable tide of chromosomal erosion will have one result: men will eventually become extinct. Now, we are not necessarily advocating such a dystopian view of the future for men, but during the course of our research over the last few years there does appear to be at least a few advantages that women have over men in a networked world – advantages which may result in a more diminished role for those of us who lack the XX edge.

Are men and women really different? Helen Fisher, an anthropologist at Rutgers University in New York, believes that they are.[3] Men, she maintains, focus on one thing at a time, always moving in a "straightforward, linear, causal path towards a specific goal: the solution." Fisher calls this "step thinking." Women, in contrast, are able to distribute their attention across a number of tasks and issues, avoiding the sharp compartmentalization of the male mind. She calls this "web thinking." Web thinking results is the capacity to see "the whole versus a focus on the parts; multi-tasking versus one thing at a time."

Professor Kathy Sykes, is a living, breathing example of a woman's proposed advantage for seeing the bigger picture. She simultaneously fills the roles of an academic, broadcaster and government advisor. In an interview with the BBC on the topic of science generally, she had this to say,

> I think in science it's really important to try to have a holistic approach. I think it's one of the problems in science today that people are really in these narrow channels and fields, and the more that you can talk with people in different disciplines you know the better you do. And it is, I think, a treat here because you've got different kinds of scientists; and so actually to solve any particular problem bringing all of those things together can be much more powerful than just, you know, say having a physicist.

It's an intriguing quote because it hints at a slightly different stance on the male-female divide. Rather than it being a question of problem analysis versus synthesis, her emphasis on the importance of people and discussion suggests the source of the gap may be more about a difference in the sort of outcomes on which men and women tend to focus. In the words of Simon Baron-Cohen, a professor in the fields of psychology and psychiatry at the University of Cambridge, men seem to have evolved a brain that is more effective at systematizing, and women have a brain that is inherently more successful at empathizing.[4]

This slight advantage leads to a difference in preference in how men and women approach their work and leadership roles.

What do the words "systematizing" and "empathizing" really mean? Baron-Cohen's describes "systematizing" as "the drive to analyse, explore and construct a system . . . This is done in order to understand and predict the system, or to invent a new one." In more general terms, this preference can manifest itself in a variety of forms from lists of birds seen on a particular journey to collecting and cataloguing books written by authors while residents of the famously bohemian Chelsea hotel in New York. "Empathizing" is, as you might expect, people-focused and involves the ability to "spontaneously and naturally tune into another person's thoughts and feelings." Baron-Cohen under-lines the importance of not only being able to understand someone else's thinking, but also to have a sense of the emotions that person might be feeling. It's a finer and more focused distinction than Helen Fisher's approach, and speaks to approaches to organizational life and leadership that we will address now.

The evidence cited by people like Fisher and Baron-Cohen is wide, varied and compelling. It includes studies on brain development that demonstrates the impact of testosterone in enhancing "systemizing" capability in the right hemisphere of the brain, a hormone that is obvi-ously more prevalent in men than women. More practically, and here's a game we can all play, Baron-Cohen and his colleague Sally Wheel-wright have designed a test for the ability to empathize.[5] It involves showing participants photographs of faces demonstrating emotion, but only revealing the section around the eyes. Generally, they found that we are all "very good at the test," but women are more accurate on this task than men. Test yourself. Most of Professor Baron-Cohen's tools are available at www.autismresearchcentre.com.

There are a couple of important points that need to be made when considering gender differences. The first, and Baron-Cohen makes this point explicitly in his book, "The Essential Difference," is that the results of investigations into the psychological and neurological differ-ences between men and women should be framed from the perspective that these trends are on an "average," and that there are exceptions to these trends. Not all women are better than men at empathizing; some men fail miserably when it comes to categorizing the world around them. Secondly, and this is an equally important point, none of this research asserts an absolute superiority of one gender over another. Investigations of this ilk are enquiries into difference, not talent.

Why might this be important for our understanding of leadership? Well, just for a second, let's return to a guiding principle of this book: the importance of context. Historically, leaders have operated in a world where we have seen organizations as machines and people as the cogs in those machines. Just the word "organization" itself is seeped in this mechanical metaphor; it is derived from the Greek word "organon" meaning tool or instrument. Classic organizational design, taking its inspiration from the military and the influence of the Scottish economist Adam Smith, has demanded that to optimize the efficiency in organizations, leaders and managers had to focus on activities such as planning, programming, command, co-ordination and control. But the world has changed. As we discussed in Chapter 2, organizations are becoming flatter in terms of their structures; and the means of production (whether of knowledge, products, services and ideas) has evolved to become more distributed. These "networked" organizations, require some of the skills that have dominated thinking for so long, but they also need vision and influence, facilitation and support. These are the skills that are much more associated with the "empathizer" or the "web thinkers" described earlier.

But let's move from the abstract to the concrete. The financial collapse of 2008/2009 claimed many victims, but you really know you're in the middle of a serious economic crisis when an entire country goes under. The meltdown of the whole Icelandic economy in 2008 was as shocking as it was unexpected; but the economic disintegration also brought about new opportunities for female business leaders in Iceland. February 2009 saw an article in a European periodical that featured some of the women making great strides in the leadership of the economy out of the financial quicksand. One interviewee, Halla Tomasdottir, a notable Icelandic business woman is one of the founders of Audur Capital, an investment fund dedicated to investing in green technology. When evaluating whether to invest in a particular venture, she emphasized the importance of assessing the "emotional capital" of the prospect company to understand whether the organizational culture is "an asset or a liability." She also asserted the importance of understanding the "payback" not just in terms of profit but also in terms of environmental and social returns. This approach of Ms Tomasdottir and her co-founders is exactly what one might expect of a psychological "type" that values the bigger picture, sees the contribution of people as something more than purely instrumental and fundamentally understands the importance of dialogue and relationships in organizations.

In Baron-Cohen's book, *"The Essential Difference"* he makes a play that "systemizers" will make better leaders than empathizers because, "a good systemiser can see people as a system . . . like cogs in a mechanical system." Baron-Cohen steers clear of making a gender preference in terms of leadership capability; Helen Fisher, on the other hand, feels restrained by no such compunction. She clearly sets out her stall that women have the potential to surpass men in terms of performance in today's complex world.

Our view of what this all means for leadership is more nuanced than a polarized view of "web thinkers" versus "step thinkers"; or "empathizers" versus "systemizers"; and certainly "men" versus "women." The truth is, in a network organization, like any organization, you need complementary skills and aptitudes to deliver results efficiently and effectively. While in a network organization, people skills and social intelligence may need to predominate; organizations do not achieve their goals through relationships alone – there is still a need to bring the skills required to organize and systemize.

And so that brings us to our own view of what we've called "network leadership," a different lens on the leadership problem. Network leadership amounts to three clusters of thinking strategies and behaviors that have proved useful for generating different types of social capital in a leadership context. We have gathered and honed these clusters during workshops, consultancy assignments, coaching sessions and one-to-ones with leaders and their people over the last five years, in assorted locations around the world. It is a structure that has grown from conversation and observation. It is not a "normative" model designed to assess leaders and produce leadership conformity: it is a framework designed to provoke debate, encourage reflection and, ultimately, inspire action.

NETWORK LEADERSHIP: CONNECT AND DELIVER!

There are three key areas to what we've called, "Network leadership." Each of the three labels, for example, "cognitive flexibility" in Figure 5.1 refers to a cluster of thinking and behavioral strategies that we've grouped from a commonsense perspective. Within each cluster, there will be a number of core elements, all of which interact. We've presented our framework as three overlapping circles to underline, again, the point about remembering the whole. Any one element of this framework is necessary for effective leadership, but it is not sufficient.

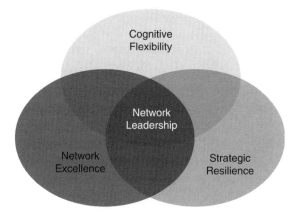

FIGURE 5.1 **Three-circle model**

Network leadership

To introduce Network leadership and to bring the model to life, we offer a short example of leadership-in-action, which demonstrates many of the elements required to connect with people and deliver great results.

For those of you who have not visited the Royal Albert Hall in London, it is a cavernous auditorium inspired by ancient amphitheatres. Its stately dome sits atop one of the most distinctive buildings in the world. The grand hall itself can accommodate approximately 8000 people, and is home to an annual British concert that heralds the end of the British summer – The Proms. In the autumn of 2001, the Institute of Directors invited a gaggle of luminaries from the business world to give their insights to the packed house at their yearly management jamboree. Present among the speakers was Sir Eddie George, at the time Governor of the Bank of England; Barbara Cassani, the founder of Go!; Hans Snook, the chairman of Orange; and Sir Christopher Evans, noted biotech entrepreneur and, at the time, advisor to Tony Blair on all things entrepreneurial.

Hans Snook gave one of the first presentations: a full-bodied, multimedia, audio-visual extravaganza that was totally in keeping with someone representing a technology organization that had always strived for a distinctive brand. It was one of those presentations that left you feeling a little bloated at the end, reminiscent of that sensation of having enjoyed a very good meal but slightly over-indulging.

91

If you looked around the auditorium, you could see there were more than a few members of the audience that would have offered a few good sales leads to get out of their seats and stretch their legs.

It was against this backdrop that Sir Christopher Evans took the platform. In 2001, Sir Christopher was in his mid-forties with a muscular frame and a red-haired ruddiness that shouts "rugby and the valleys." Welsh through and through, he was born in Port Talbot, a small town in South Wales, noted more for heavy industry than as a breeding ground for visionary and driven entrepreneurs. Having successfully started and sold a number of biotech companies, he had founded and was Chairman of Merlin Biosciences, a venture capital firm dedicated to medical sciences. He is a man that can't help but look forward with an optimistic glint in his eye.

As he settled himself behind the podium, a member of the event's organization team came hurriedly and nervously onto the stage and whispered something into his ear. The entire audience could see that something was not quite right. The entrepreneur hesitated for just a second before turning to the audience with a wide smile and saying in his sonorous Celtic lilt: "Well, I'm buggered! My slides don't work!" His relaxed style and language contrasted with the formality of the event, a major landmark in the British business calendar. That, combined with the notion of a failed PowerPoint presentation, particularly after the Snook technology show, resulted in a wave of laughter and some spontaneous applause. He hadn't even started.

The Welsh have a reputation for being great storytellers. Sir Christopher didn't disappoint. And he didn't need visual aids to grip his audience: "This is the most important presentation you're going to hear today. Why? Because it's about life and death, particularly yours in the front row." It was a startling opening. He blasted through the next forty-five minutes with an extemporized series of anecdotes and opinions, leaving the safety of his script behind and ignoring the security blanket of the slides, which eventually appeared. His topics ranged from the inadequacies of cloning technology to the phenomenal promise of stem cell research. In a sense, it was a sales pitch; but a sales pitch that cut a swathe through some complex topics without succumbing to lazy intellectualism or the carelessly abstract. His story was relevant, real and meaningful to everyone in a room that had suddenly become very small.

This forty-five minute slice of leadership life captures many of the elements we believe are essential for connecting with people and delivering great results.

- **Cognitive flexibility** has two core ingredients, which are a mind that thrives on complexity and the ability to reduce something complex to the readily comprehensible. Sir Christopher's presentation condensed twenty-five years' experience as businessman, entrepreneur and scientist into forty-five minutes; he pithily cut through the arcane world of biotechnology and told an engaging story that didn't require a PhD in Biochemistry to understand and was relevant to everyone in the Albert Hall. Aside from these aspects, cognitive flexibility is, in a sense, the "engine room" for the next two capability clusters.
- **Network excellence** has a number of elements, all of which are important strands in the development of social capital. A number of these network behaviors were apparent during this session, including the ability to demonstrate warmth and empathy; an ability to identify common ground with a diverse group of people and a capacity to project real confidence when meeting people for the first time. Of course, there are other elements to this particular "capability" that we will address later in this chapter.
- **Strategic resilience** involves three crucial aspects of leadership – a focus on outcomes, a combination of optimism and flexibility in achieving those outcomes and releasing energy. Some of the successful leaders we have interviewed and worked with during our careers are almost pathologically focused on outcomes, both medium and long-term. That intense focus is accompanied by an incredible sense that any outcome is possible with the right degree of energy and flexibility. During Sir Christopher's presentation, he painted an exciting picture of several long-term outcomes that would have been of genuine interest to potential investors or the casual observer. What was most striking about our Welsh orator was the way in which he engaged his audience with a level of aspiration and "possibility" about the biotechnology sector that seemed to teeter on the incredible, but which you believed was possible.

NETWORK LEADERSHIP: A DEEPER DIVE

Cognitive flexibility

As we have outlined, cognitive flexibility is all about the human capacity for adapting our thinking strategies to face new and unanticipated challenges in the environment. This enables us not just to cope with the complex world we live in, but to thrive in it. This is a facet of the human mind that is still poorly understood. Here is a more formal and thorough definition:

> By cognitive flexibility, we mean the ability to spontaneously restructure one's knowledge, in many ways, in adaptive response to radically changing situational demands. (Cognitive flexibility) enables understanding to develop in interconnected web-like structures which will give greater flexibility in the way it is applied.
>
> (Spiro 1992)[6]

In a way, the "web-like structures" that Spiro proposes for cognitive flexibility echo the web of connections we suggest are useful for developing social capital in the world. That richness of inter-connection enables an individual to avoid becoming trapped in a particular thought "silo"; to address a challenge or a problem from different angles; and to adjust analysis and decision making quickly in the light of new information. Cognitive flexibility is exactly the opposite of what is encouraged and developed at some business schools where each faculty "temple" demands devotion to their particular perspective: the supply chain faculty believes inventory and logistics are the solution to all problems; the finance guys know that it's all about the numbers; while the "people people" (the HR crowd) repeatedly espouse the one fundamental of all businesses – it's all about the people.

Cognitive flexibility is, in part, what Professor Roger Martin of the Toronto School of Business has in mind in his book *The Opposable Mind*.[7] Martin's view is that successful leaders are able to hold in mind two opposing options and to create a third, more effective option, which still contains elements of the previous two options. He cites a useful example of this in an online interview with a journalist from *Business Week*.[8] His illustration of "the opposable mind" centers on A J. Lafley, the man who became CEO of Procter & Gamble (P&G) in 2000. At the time, P&G faced a number of challenges, not least of which was how to harness innovation more effectively across the organization. Lafley was faced with what appeared to be two stark choices: take a "business as usual" approach to innovation, with all the high costs associated with existing innovation practices; alternatively, he could cut back expenditure and reduce innovation practices across the P&G footprint. Roger Martin regards this as a classic opposable mind dilemma – the stark choice between two fundamentally different choices. Instead of succumbing to the lobbyists on either side of the argument, Lafley found a "third way." He insisted that rather than driving innovation internally, he would insist that at least 50 percent of new products should come from outside the organization. He called this program "connect and develop." The program was a major success for P&G.

Yet another suggestion of the importance of "cognitive flexibility" came through a research program of high-performing organizations carried out by The Work Foundation.[9] In a sense, this was a traditional study of what makes organizations perform better than others – and the results are what you would expect from many of these type of studies: the importance of people, innovation, customers, etc. However, it did produce one unique, provocative finding. According to this piece of research, what differentiated high-performing organizations from "mediocre" or "poor" performing organizations was the capability to manage the tensions and the "trade-offs" that inevitably occur on a daily basis for many of the leaders within the organization. Leaders who endowed their organizations with a sort of intellectual nimbleness resulted in higher levels of productivity and growth.

Leadership, complexity and meaning

Clare Chapman is Director General of Workforce for the NHS and Social Care in England. To put the size of that seemingly innocuous word "workforce" into perspective, the NHS is the third largest employer in the world after the Chinese Red Army and the Indian Railways. It's a job where it might be easy to become submerged in the size and complexity of the organization, but Ms Chapman is no stranger to that level of organizational intricacy, having been Group HR Director for Tesco at the time of rapid international expansion. When we discussed this issue with her in her Whitehall office she had this to say.

A major mindset shift for me in this role has been from leading within a single organisation to leading within a sector. The NHS is no longer a single, monolithic organisation. There are millions of moving parts across the healthcare sector with independent as well as NHS organisations serving the health needs of their communities.

They are linked by a shared commitment to high quality care, as described this year in the NHS Constitution.

Good leaders create meaning. Shared values and a constant painting of the common purpose in a way that engages with citizens and staff can help collaboration happen. One of my roles is to continuously reinforce that common meaning. Our values are real. Tangible. They have been identified through consultation with patients, staff, public and practitioners. Not just a well meaning but superficial exercise by a group of executives in a top floor meeting room. So we know that we all understand, support and mean to live by those values, we relate everything in some way back to those values. We can help ourselves to have a smaller rule book. It is a core language that we can all speak – the one that does not need constant translation.

In a sense, what Ms Chapman is describing is the ability to turn complex situations into compelling narratives – in short, "storytelling." Dan Pink, author of *Whole New Mind* and ex-speechwriter for Vice-President Al Gore, had this to say about the importance of storytelling: "People who ignore the importance of storytelling today do so at their own personal and professional peril."[10] His argument is that, in today's non-stop, boundaryless world, there is an imperative to make sense of that world, to simplify and to express ourselves in ways that really connect with people. Or in the words of Robert McKee, advisor to successful scriptwriters all over the world, "A story weaves together facts and events in a way that leaves an indelible impression on our hearts and minds."[11]

Organizational storytelling is much in vogue. Business leaders, "gurus," psychologists and professional storytellers from a range of backgrounds, including the theatre, have enhanced the profile of this cross-cultural, creative and timeless art. And there is persuasive evidence that stories do have a telling impact on organizations.

e2v is a hi-tech manufacturing company that provides components and subsystems for a range of applications that stretch from the Hubble telescope to thermal imaging cameras to sophisticated cancer treatment devices. They have been developing communication and leadership skills through storytelling. Why? It's a question that, when put to Peter Scraton, the Group HR Director, he addressed with tough honesty and infectious enthusiasm: "Story telling is a core leadership skill. It's about making sense of the world and engaging other people with that vision. The great unravelling of the world's economy in 2008 and 2009 demands that people in leadership roles creatively find a way to understand our new commercial environment, and to instil in others a positive sense of our future. The tools and techniques of story creation and story telling are essential for leaders to achieve those goals." e2v's commitment to storytelling finds use in a number of ways, including developing team identity and helping leaders engage their staff more effectively through the use of engaging narratives.

In the context of network leadership, storytelling is highly relevant. Researchers have found that stories themselves can be highly effective tools to influence and persuade others. Associate Professor Jennifer Edson Escalas, in a marketing study for the Vanderbilt School of Management, demonstrated that test audiences react more positively to advertisements presented in story form than to those presented in a format that sets our arguments for the product.[12] Her explanation is that when listening to stories our critical faculties are dulled and we become more personally involved with the product through the story itself. In general terms, psychologists tend to explain this sort of result as a consequence of the essentially social nature of storytelling. Storytellers need to invoke powers of empathy to create stories that engage, while listening to stories often involves personal identification with a combination of the story and the storyteller. So it would seem that when either bridging or bonding, stories are a great tool for leaders in many different situations.

Strategic resilience

Organizations are intended as a hymn to efficiency; but too often they become no more than a broken chorus of pointless bureaucracy. When the tension between purpose and bureaucratic process breaks in favor of the latter, you know a few things about that organization: firstly, it will be stuffed to the gills with people who have lost their focus on results; secondly, it's an organization in a state of inevitable demise; and lastly, the leaders have long since departed. Leadership is nothing if it is not about delivering outcomes. The inescapable, incontrovertible and universal fact of leadership is that leaders have to be resolutely focused on aligning their people with delivering outcomes, measured in whatever way is relevant and appropriate. Everything discussed in the name of leadership is ultimately in the service of delivering those outcomes.

"It is our attitude at the beginning of a difficult task which, more than anything, will affect its outcome." So said the venerable psychologist William James during the late nineteenth century, and from the point of view of our work over the last several years, the same is true today. To be more precise there appears to be three central psychological factors that play a role in achieving the goals we have set for ourselves: "realistic optimism," "outcome focus" and "releasing energy." Let's briefly examine the second of these three factors before taking a longer look at the other two.

Peter Lidstone, one of our key case studies, had this to say about the importance of outcomes when trying to align thousands of people in manufacturing facilities all round the world:

> Outcomes are what leadership is all about. You can talk about networks and storytelling and relationships, but if you don't know where you're going, or why you're going there, it's all just a nice game. It feels good and everyone is happy, but there is no real outcome, and ultimately no real sense of satisfaction. I have always thought of myself as an "operator" at the core, not a great "strategic thinker," not a great artist. But that means even at a very senior level I have the purpose – and the outcome – at the front of my mind at all times. My role is to communicate this again and again. And to communicate it in different ways to different people, but to do it unerringly until it is achieved.

For those people who are genuinely outcome focused, like Peter Lidstone, it takes the form of, if not an obsession, then certainly something that occupies their thinking for the most part of every day. Is there a danger that this leads to perfectionism? When talking to us, Clare Chapman had this to say about "outcomes" and whether this leads to a fixation on perfectionism:

> For me, it's all about urgency. Urgency is critical – don't wait until tomorrow just because it's too complicated or too hard. I like the mantra of "be better today than we were yesterday" improving things for patients and staff whilst respecting value for money. Healthcare is happening now: the patients, the families, the professionals that we are all accountable to are experiencing this now, today. Don't let perfection stand in the way of improvement.

Another pitfall that some leaders fall into when looking to achieve specific outcomes is that they become too fixed on how to get there. Typically, this takes the form of a deep reliance on strategic planning processes that provide step-by-step roadmaps to a "Promised Land." The inherent dangers of dependence upon the stalwarts of strategic planning, spreadsheets and process charts, have been pointed out in Henry Mintzberg's, *The Rise and Fall of Strategic Planning* in which he lambasts organizations that are process heavy and vision-light.[13] He argues that some strategies should be no more than a vision in order to provide space for flexibility and adaptability. One of Mintzberg's more challenging ideas for leaders and their organizations is that strategy may be emergent; variables such as the economic environment, the skills and availability of people, together with general market trends will vary over time and require leaders to adapt accordingly. Outcome focus, as proposed here, readily accepts the need for flexibility when moving toward the aim of an ultimate objective. The people interviewed for this book, and the leaders with whom we have worked in the past, have all demonstrated exactly that sort of flexibility.

Realistic optimism

A family had twin boys whose only resemblance to each other was their looks. If one felt it was too hot, the other thought it was too cold. If one said the TV was too loud, the other claimed the volume needed to be turned up. Opposite in every way, one was an eternal optimist, the other a doom and gloom pessimist. Just to see what would happen, on the twins' birthday their father loaded the pessimist's room with every imaginable toy and game. The optimist's room he loaded with horse manure. That night the father passed by the pessimist's room and found him sitting amid his new gifts crying bitterly. "Why are you crying?" the father asked. "Because my friends will be jealous, I'll have to read all these instructions before I can do anything with this stuff, I'll constantly need batteries, and my toys will eventually get broken" answered the pessimist twin. Passing the optimist twin's room, the father found him dancing for joy in the pile of manure. "What are you so happy about?" he asked. To which his optimist twin replied, "There's got to be a pony in here somewhere!"

This old joke about the difference between optimists and pessimists goes to the heart of a really important facet of leadership: the fundamental ability to overcome obstacles and adversity with a healthy dose of optimism. When we say "optimism" we mean a general tendency to expect a positive outcome, but we're not talking about the blind faith of a young Candide. The young boy's hope for a pony was not without basis; he did have some pretty irrefutable evidence that some sort of equine presence wasn't far away! Similarly, the leaders we interviewed have all shown a clear-sighted understanding of the world around them, complemented by a logical and irresistible view of the future.

In the Spring of 2009, we met with Stewart Milne, hugely successful entrepreneur and Chairman of a large construction company based in Scotland. With the dust of the economic collapse still swirling around us, and as someone running a business at the sharp end of the economy, he had this to say about what the future held for house building specifically and construction generally: "There is a way forward for us and for any company that sticks at it. I don't know exactly what that way forward looks like, but I know it's there – we just have to find it. Of course we have to look after the present – cut costs, implement process efficiencies, reduce inventory and materials etc, but this is also a great time to reinvent ourselves and how we do things so that we can continue growing." Mr Milne was under no illusions about the present. He acknowledged the turmoil surrounding him and his industry. But he looked forward with a realistic optimism that never allowed him to lose faith in the possibility of the organization achieving their goals with the right amount of hard work and ingenuity.

Part of the skill set of the realistically optimistic appears to be the ability to reinterpret a situation and reframe the world. There can be no greater test of this aspect of realistic optimism than the concentration camps of Nazi Germany. Viktor Frankl, neurologist and psychiatrist, found himself in various camps between 1942 and 1945, including Theresienstadt and Auschwitz. Aside from his own suffering at the hands of the Nazis, Frankl's wife was sent to Belsen where she was killed; and his parents to Auschwitz where they were also murdered. Despite the horrors of this phase of his life, Frankl remained sane and hopeful by finding meaning in his experiences, ultimately developing his thinking into a systematic form of psychotherapy called "logotherapy." Frankl offers a primary example of finding meaning in the midst of the seemingly meaningless in his book *Man's Search for Meaning*.[14] He tells of a situation where, when faced with more senseless brutality at the hands of a sadistic supervisor, he committed himself to giving lectures on the psychology of concentration camps when, and if, he was released. He gave himself specific goals in the future than enabled him to create real meaning from the present.

Stewart Milne, the house-building entrepreneur, did exactly that during the conversation described earlier. Instead of focusing on collapsing house prices, the disappearance of capital for new mortgages or even the inability of record low interest rates in the UK to restart the market, Stewart reframed the world so that he saw it as providing fresh opportunity and new impetus for him and his orgranization. To some extent, the unprecedented economic challenges appeared to bring fresh energy and zeal to his view of his company's long-term prospects, and how he and his senior team might change practices for the better.

Engaging others and releasing energy

Regardless of how "outcome focused" or "emotionally resilient" leaders are, they cannot achieve ambitious goals by themselves. A leader has to engage others and find ways to release their energy and talents in what has to be a common pursuit. As Peter Lidstone, European Supply Chain Director at Akzonobel Decorative Paints, pointed out strongly on several occasions: "[Y]ou just can't do it all by yourself. However many hours you put in, you have to draw on not just the skills and knowledge, but the commitment and effort of other people. You would think this is obvious, but I've lost count of how many senior executives I've seen who hold onto stuff too long because they don't trust other people to do it for them."

So once a manager has grasped this simple principle, how does he or she elicit that commitment and release that energy? From talking to leaders and their people, many of the behaviors are what you would expect for this aspect of leadership: communicating the vision and purpose clearly; motivating people with balanced feedback delivered at the right time and in the right way; involving others' decisions and plans. Perhaps what is less obvious is the reciprocity that is required. Back to Peter Lidstone: "You don't get others to work for you, really work for you, unless they see this as a mutual investment. It's a two way relationship that is built on trust." Asked how, in a practical sense he achieves this he replied, "I enable people to make the connection between their role and delivering value to the organisation. That's not easy in the complex and often changing structures we operate. I need to keep it clear and simple, and make sure I spell out the very real difference our *success* [his emphasis] makes to the organization overall. Then they all begin to feel needed and that they can have an impact on the organisation overall." Peter Lidstone operates in a complex, but not uncommon structure within the private sector. How do these principles apply elsewhere?

The Cheltenham Science Festival is a major event in the timetable for Public Science in the United Kingdom. Started in 2002, it has quickly established itself as the most significant event of its kind, directed and attended by a glittering array of world-class scientists and respected leaders and business people. In 2009 these included Lord Robert Winston, Richard Dawkins, Sir Richard Branson, chef Heston Blumenthal and politician David Cameron among many others. The festival's intended audience seems to be everyone, from children to grandparents, from the serious science buff to the enthusiastic amateur. Kathy Sykes, one of our interviewees, is one of the festival's creators and directors and waxed lyrical about its range and quality of content, including in the 2009 program, sessions on "climate change and personal responsibility," "Good Bugs and Bad Bugs" and "penisology." With any event of this size, success is dependent upon the commitment and effort of a wide range of people. The Science Festival is no exception and a key ingredient of its success is the volunteers who dedicate a significant amount of their personal time. This is what Kathy has to say about how she "releases energy" in her volunteer army:

> My role is to connect the volunteers to the scientists, to the organisers, to the public and to each other. We have a pre-festival dinner especially for the volunteers which I see as crucial for me to attend and speak to each of them. This is not just to thank them, but to help them understand what a critical role they play, and how this contributes to all the other players. This makes all the difference – it enables people to take ownership and feel a real sense of responsibility and pride. The word volunteer fails to capture their energy and value to the event . . . we simply could not do it without them. Nor would we want to.

Professor Sykes' approach has many similarities with Peter Lidstone's leadership style; it is involving, based on enabling everyone to understand how they contribute to the end result, and is clearly reciprocal. To sum up, leaders like Kathy Sykes and Peter Lidstone engage their people. And engaging other people ends the second leg of our leadership model, moving us finally into the third and final element – the importance of people, networks and ultimately social capital.

Network excellence

And so to our final element: Network excellence. From our vantage point in the "cheap seats," the leadership literature has not paid sufficient attention to this area. However, as we have argued throughout this book, the nature and quality of our connection to other people goes to the heart of how leaders make decisions and achieve their results. Network excellence has three core constituents that vary in importance depending on context and the exact nature of the social capital a leader may want to develop. Those three constituents are: Network Sustainer; Network Builder and Network Architect. We will bring each constituent to life through the real examples offered to us by leaders in a variety of settings, roles and organizations.

Network Sustainer

These are the leaders that, regardless of obstacles, maintain strong relationships with a core set of people over extended periods of time. These leaders are supportive and generally good at sharing information to people within that network (although they may be selective about who becomes part of their network initially). Once this has happened the network sustainer will demonstrate warmth and real interest in people. They tend to be great confidantes and are regarded as being extremely trustworthy.

Ieda Gomes is VP of New Ventures within British Petroleum (BP). She is Brazilian by birth and international in approach. She studied chemical engineering in Brazil, as one of only 17 women in a class of 50. She then moved to Switzerland to complete her masters degree and has been on the move constantly ever since. She is currently based in the United Kingdom and we were fortunate to be able to speak to her there.

Relationships are at the heart of how I approach my role. If some-body needs my help, regardless of whether it's part of my perform-ance contract; I try to give them support. I have many long-term relationships within and outside of my employer, which span several roles across my career. My view is that you never know when some-one will be able to offer you critical advice and/or support. Nor when that flow may work in reverse. On a large or small scale, that is the grandest feeling.

No one would doubt the intrinsic wisdom of Ieda's words, but main-taining that level of emotional connection to someone requires an investment of time and effort when there may not be an obvious return on that investment. Ieda recognizes the challenges of her approach, but gives a clear warning about taking a short-term view of our relationships:

Sustaining relationships over time can be a real challenge – especially when you are working across functional, time, geographical, and cultural barriers. But if you don't maintain at least a core of these within your network – relationships that give you or require you to give immediate access to trusted advice and support – you feel that an important part of your life may be missing. They are your "safety line" when all else feels uncertain and lonely. And you have to earn those relationships – you cannot take them for granted. We are all busy and in demand. If you do not respect these relationships over all others, why should they respect you?

Ieda is a leader who implicitly recognizes the importance of prioritiz-ing our relationships. Her approach is not based on advocating the investment of time and energy into an entire network from casual acquaintances to close working colleagues, but rather – as Ms Gomes describes – a "core" set of important relationships. These people may be the immediate members of a formal team. Alternatively they could be part of an informal network that still constitutes a critical group of people that work together on a project-by-project or activity set basis. And this is where real judgment and, if you like, social "intel-ligence" plays a role. All of our research indicates that, when prioritiz-ing our relationships, we cannot adopt a ruthlessly utilitarian view of the people we want to include in our network. It's imperative that we retain a healthy and genuine interest in those people. It requires a combination of the "common purpose" and respect that Will Hutton underlined in Chapter 3.

But leaders have to avoid falling into the "cosy clique" with their networks. Or in the words of Ieda Gomes:

> "Any network needs oxygen" – that is, a flow of new people and ideas over established friendships and trusted colleagues. Without this you feel cosy – but the air gets stale. You have to open yourselves to the risk of this. It can sometimes feel uncomfortable or threatening – but without it you suffocate gently but surely. I also advise people that I am mentoring to go out and develop external relationships and external networks – they provide oxygen and different perspectives to your life and your career."

Network builder

In sharp contrast to the Network Sustainer is the entrepreneurial Network Builder. These leaders continuously and proactively extend the reach and the breadth of their network contacts. Successful network builders are likely to locate and engage with people beyond the boundaries that traditionally constrain relationship formation, for example, organizational, technical, functional, geographical and cultural boundaries. For the extreme network builder, the contacts and relationships that form part of their address book typically will span a diverse array of people, professions, talents and interests. As an example, Ieda Gomes cannot rest on the laurels of her existing contacts. She talked passionately about the need for fresh network connections:

> I always work on the adage – Be curious. Never rest your mind; the world is an immense library where you learn every day. My contacts – my colleagues, my friends and my business partners are doors into that library"
>
> My external relationships are as important as my internal ones. We partner on many of our ventures, and I am an active member in many industry committees and organisations. This is an indispensable aspect of my role. I cannot deliver without it. And it is dynamic. The network of people that I need to hook up with changes constantly. People enter and leave the domain that I need to be a part of – and I need to be aware and active in that process. I could say

that a lot of that is about conscious scanning and monitoring of what is going on around the world – but it's more natural and … fun than that. These are real relationships and real people. So it happens through my interest in keeping in contact with them, and finding out their news as much as anything else.

The ongoing development of new relationships begs the question: how can it be done without appearing contrived or coldly intentional? Back to Ms Gomes:

Through establishing common interests. That is rarely difficult but often surprising. You think from someone's job title or biography that they might be able to help you with one thing – but when you talk to them you realise that you have a mutual challenge that can be better solved by helping each other. You don't go looking for it – it emerges through mutually sharing your own interests, goals and challenges.

What network builders don't do, and avoid doing it with real success, is to fall into the trap of making assumptions about people – something that we are as likely to do for those people we have known for years as for those people that we may have met for the first time today. While the heuristic value of people assumptions may be of value in certain situations, they can get in the way of developing great networks.

Network Architect

We tend to think about network development from a rather egocentric perspective; we all believe ourselves to be the center of our social universe. During the research and the writing of this book, we discovered something about effective leaders: often they pay as much attention, and sometimes more, to the networks and social capital of other people as they do to their own. Leaders who exhibit the behaviors of what we have called "network architect" introduce others into their own network, connections that are formed to benefit the other person exclusively and occasionally for mutual benefit. These leaders will champion and support other people, conferring on them credibility and a form of reputational social capital through their patronage. And it doesn't stop there. We have found network architects who encourage people to share ideas and thoughts across networks, always ensuring that these individuals receive acknowledgment and credit. In short, they help other people develop their own networks and are trusted by those people to have their best interests at heart.

Peter Scraton is a poacher–turned-gamekeeper. Having completed his Masters degree in industrial relations at the London School of Economics during the late 1980's, he moved into a series of trade union roles before changing careers and becoming a member of the human resources profession. Having learnt the black arts of HR in organisations such as PepsiCo, Heinz and 02, he has some interesting observations about the importance of "network architecture" within successful organisations. In the situations Peter describes, network architecture is brought about not for the benefit of Peter, or any one individual, but for the success of the organization as a whole. He explained this further when he was talking to us:

> A particular challenge for organisations, particularly as a business grows within increasingly global and competitive markets, is acquisition and then the subsequent integration of new companies. This is a notoriously difficult and risky time, as processes and cultures come head to head. I learned a long time ago that you don't acquire, or merge, companies. Instead you open up the opportunity to merge teams of highly talented, but potentially temperamental individuals. You can only do that by enabling the development of relationships built upon respect and – ultimately – trust. A critical part of my role is to help build those bridges – often during turbulent and uncertain times. And clearly I can't do that on my own. I need to call upon people in my own team and the wider organisation to reach out and start to form the framework of that new set of connections. Facilitating that is a critical first step – and often one that can make the difference between success and failure.

One of the most striking and inspiring examples of a leader acting as a network architect came from Professor Kathy Sykes, when we met up with her in her unassuming garret office in Bristol. Here she is describing how her role in developing the public engagement in science goes from what seems to be a terribly worthy but abstract goal to something real and concrete through developing connections between unlikely groups of people:

> It is very easy to take the notion of "Public Engagement in Science" down the easy route – engage with open-minded science teachers at

well-run and well-funded schools, or adults already keen to discuss science and ideas. But that is too obvious and not what I think the role is about. Instead, I wanted to explore how the university might engage a community we're not usually good at reaching. And how we might do that – according to the community's interests, not ours. Working with Explore (a science discovery centre that Kathy helped to create in Bristol) and a community worker, we aimed to reach the St Paul's community within Bristol.

St Pauls, an inner suburb at the heart of Bristol, has a vibrant Afro-Caribbean community but is more often remembered for a series of flashpoint riots in the 1980's. Described in Wikipedia as characterized by "neglect, crime and a pervasive drug culture" it is hardly an obvious venue for scientific debate.

The first step of course was to go to that community and ask what they might like to talk to us about. After some discussion, the answer was: "Do drugs do your head in." I knew that all of my preconceptions about how to set up such a debate were almost certainly doomed to failure, so I put them firmly aside and we consciously continued to ask questions and – listen. We worked closely with local people, including some Rastafarians who helped to make all the decisions about location (local community centres), ads for the event (on an illegal, pirate radio station "Passion FM" by them (not me in my posh voice)), and timing (early evening). Without many of their deep insights we would have had an empty room full of anxious academics with no one to talk with.

Instead we ran a series of public meetings with a range of people, including neuroscientists, psychologists, social scientists, local community leaders, Rastafarians and a government adviser on drug classification. The audience was about half black, half white and included concerned citizens, parents, teachers, drug users and even a drug dealer. I have to be honest – at times there was massive suspicion and mutual discomfort on all sides. In all the events we planned a 30-minute chill out and chat time – which turned out to really help diffuse tensions and help people listen. In one of these, we were delighted to see that a white woman who had shouted at one of the Rastafarians, was now being given advice by him on better ways of handling her drug-using son. But it was made clear from the outset that everyone had a voice and a right to speak. And we held it together. The debate was of an order that I have rarely heard before or since. A critical part was the visible listening from scientific advisers and experts – they shifted from educators to learners on an equal footing. One of the scientists there who advises the government on drug classification said he heard perspectives he'd never heard or considered before. Many of the audience and the panel told us afterwards that they had come away with not just a greater understanding of the issue, but of their wider community and their part within it. Within the academic community it can be a real challenge to shift the culture to one that values and prioritises real engagement with the public. The event was internationally recognised, and the New Zealand Government asked for a transcript of the event when making decisions on its own drug classification approaches. A primary role for me then is to help staff and students to engage effectively with the public by providing them with opportunities to do this easily, safely and in a mutually rewarding way.

FINAL THOUGHTS: SQUARING CIRCLES AND PRAISING WINE

We started this book by attacking the notion of the individual leader and asserting the importance of context and connections. We are conscious that in devoting this chapter to a model of leadership – albeit one that is not conceived in entirely normative terms – it may appear that we have lost sight of that original line of argument. So before moving on to talk about the development of leaders, we want to square the circle, or circles, of network leadership and reinforce our original thoughts.

Firstly, the concept of "network excellence" is fundamental to leadership. Everything that leaders think, do or aspire to is mediated through the thoughts and actions of others with whom they interact. Those invisible lines of connection are undeniable and impossible to ignore. Although it might have been an interesting intellectual exercise to write a book exclusively about the network elements of leadership, the truth is that research and experience have taught us that what we have called "cognitive flexibility" and "strategic resilience" are inextricably interwoven with our ability to build relationships: a triple helix of capability that captures the effective "DNA" of leadership. But, just as the successful and enduring expression of any DNA is a function of the interplay between its elements and the environment, it's also true that effective leadership in any given context, depends on the subtle predominance of certain elements over others.

We began this chapter with wine, so it's not inappropriate to finish on the same theme. If the reader has ever visited Cape Town in South Africa, you will know that it is a small city blessed with great people, stunning mountains, magnificent oceans and some of the finest vineyards in the world. There is a certain vineyard in the heartland of South African wine, a region known as Stellenbosch, where for a few South African rands, you can savor an assortment of delicious wines. The sommelier in the vineyard's restaurant plays an enlightening trick for those people who enjoy wine, but are not used to the gustatory analysis of a more experienced palate. He will offer you a brief taste of two beautiful and very different red wines: one is velvet, rich and smooth; while the second wine is earthy, almost gritty and very spicy. He will then question you about why you think the two wines differ so much. For the naïve taste bud, the answer seems obvious – the grapes are different. In fact, as he takes great joy in explaining, the grapes are absolutely identical. They are grown for exactly the same time and are fermented and bottled with a similar process. The difference? It's the environment or the "terroir." Each grape is grown about twenty miles apart but in soils that differ significantly in the mineral content and the slope of the land. The results are equally enjoyable, though the environment has shaped very different results. We cannot forget that our three circles will manifest themselves very differently in the world depending on the context and the pattern of social connections a leader has around her. It is misguided enthusiasm, or just plainly wrong, to become overly focused on any specific areas. As Professor Feynman reminded us, although we may have segmented leadership into so many convenient elements, we have to put it all back together again in order to make sense of, and really appreciate, great leadership.

6

THE LIGHT BULB ILLUSION

The yellow ambience of the Broadway theater lights dimmed slowly until we sat in perfect darkness. Moments later, a single bulb from a powerful stage light illuminated an actor who stood in the center stage looking out toward the audience. Dressed in a sober, gray pin-striped suit with a conservative red tie, a smart white handkerchief placed neatly into his breast pocket, and which alluded to an earlier age, he addressed the invisible full house. With a few pithy, energetic sentences, the actor's character points out that it is only the light reflecting off him that makes him visible to the audience. At the time it seems an unnecessary, self-evident truth.

Now a theater on Broadway may not be the obvious place to start a chapter for a book on leadership. But it is the performance of a play in New York's famous theater strip that will set the tone for next twenty or so pages. The play is *The Farnsworth Invention* written by Aaron Sorkin, better known for his creation of *The West Wing*, a TV social drama about privileged and brilliant staffers in the West Wing of a contemporary and imaginary, democratic president. *The Farnsworth Invention* is a creatively licensed interpretation about real-life inventor Philo Farnsworth, who was responsible for taking an important step in the invention of television.[1] It is the opening moment's theatrical illusion of solitude, created by a single beam of stage lighting, that captures the essence of this chapter's story. Speaking about the invention of television, the lone character informs the audience that in 1921, when the play opens, no individual had the solution to the conundrum of transmitting images across distances large or small. Why is the start of this Broadway show so important to the core theme of this chapter? Part of the answer lies in Philo Farnsworth's story.

Born in 1906, Farnsworth was a precocious and precious talent that found his inspiration in science and engineering and with an eye to emulate the success of his hero Thomas Edison. When still very young he had a visionary insight into the problems of projecting images across a distance. Using his natural aptitude for engineering, Farnsworth created a device that used a vacuum tube with a lens at one end, which had a photoelectric plate for converting light to electricity, immediately in front of it. Then he created another device to read the electrical image line by line. It was 1927, and in one sense, the twenty-one-year-old Farnsworth had invented television.

From a very different perspective, Farnsworth had not invented television – there were other people in the world working on the same engineering challenge and whose ideas and inspiration derived from similar lines to young Farnsworth. David Sarnoff, Head of RCA, perhaps the most pre-eminent electronics company in the whole of America at the time, had hired scores of brilliant electrical engineers to find a solution to the vision-at-a-distance problem, not least of which was Vladimir Zworykin, a PhD physicist from Russia. As Sarnoff, who is the lone character on the stage, says in the play "no body had it," that is, there was no single individual who had complete intellectual mastery and ownership over this emerging field. In the play, Sorkin plays loosely with historical fact, but creates an endgame where, though a little industrial espionage on the part of Sarnoff and not a little hubris from Farnsworth, RCA wins the race to a fully working patent with all the riches and recognition that went with it. In reality, Farnsworth had been offered a job by Sarnoff to come and work at the RCA laboratories, but Farnsworth believed "he had it" and opted to take the route of the lone inventor. Ultimately, Farnsworth couldn't compete with the power of a company like RCA and his name is consigned to a footnote in history. He died an alcoholic at the age of sixty-four with the bitterness of defeat in his mouth. The point here is that the notion of the "lone inventor" is something of a myth – innovation is a team sport – and perhaps nowhere is this demonstrated more clearly than in the case of Philo's hero, Thomas Edison and the invention of the light bulb.

The *New York Times* is a venerable and widely respected newspaper. Established in 1851, by the early twentieth century it had established itself as an authoritative and respected voice both in the United States and abroad. In 1931, the *New York Times* published Thomas Edison's obituary and had this to say about him:

Edison was a solitary genius revolutionising the world and making an invisible force do his bidding – a genius that conquered conservatism ... and created wonders that transcended the predictions of utopian poets.

Fueled by such lyrical views of human beings, a picture of a light bulb has become the classic, if not clichéd, symbolic image of the "eureka" moment, the instant when an idea is purported to arrive almost magically in the mind of the inventor. However, if we take a closer look at the history of the light bulb, and the life of Mr Edison, we can begin to see that the "light bulb illusion" is something akin to the "leadership illusion," the tendency to attribute successes entirely to the capabilities of a single individual.

The story of the incandescent light bulb is not as straightforward as we like to think. According to historians, there is a long list of inventors of incandescent lamps before the arrival of Mr Thomas Edison onto the scene. Often these inventors were working on the same problems at the same time, lodging patents for similar inventions within weeks of each other. Edison's success was in producing the first commercially viable light bulb that was relatively cheap to produce and which had significant durability. In *Edison's Electric Light: Biography of an Invention*, published in 1987 by three historians Robert Friedel, Paul Israel and Bernard Finn, the authors argue that Edison's success lay in his canny combination of three factors: an effective incandescent material that lasted over time (he found that carbonized bamboo could last for 1200 hours); the ability to sustain a higher vacuum than others, avoiding the rapid blackening of the bulb; and a lamp that made power distribution from a central source economically practical.[2] In short, it wasn't just the light itself that made his bulb a success that lives on in our memories, but an entire lighting system that solved all the problems. Edison's enduring personal success can be attributed to a number of key factors, which can be clearly seen through the lens of the network leadership model.

Firstly, in terms of **cognitive flexibility**, Edison never became encased in any specific technical specialism. This is in part attributable to his education and in part to his temperament. His formal education consisted of a short dip into the pool of public education, which lasted no more than a few weeks, followed by an extended period of home schooling with his mother, combined with an ambitious and hungry reading habit, fuelled by his own wide range of interests that included, but was not exclusive to, the subject of Science. Thomas Edison did not attend university, but as early as the age of fourteen pursued entrepreneurial ventures in printing and publishing. He then moved into telegraphy as a very young man, having been taught the essentials of this new technology from the Father of a young boy who Edison saved from injury at a railway station. In parallel with his job as a "brass pounder" (telegraph operator), Edison continued his own experiments in the hope of coming up with an invention of his own that would make him some real money. His wide interests and agile mind ultimately led to filing over a 1000 patents during his lifetime.

However, it was not just his intellectual nimbleness and web of interests that gave him success, but his real **strategic resilience**. Edison was extremely outcome focused. Edison did not invent for the sake of invention. He was focused on creating new inventions that were both practical and commercial. This focus served as a filter and a compass for his ambition and his drive. He did not allow himself to be deterred by setbacks or problems. He tackled such challenges with commitment and fortitude, but never lost sight of the need to bring new inventions into the world that would be perceived as having real value.

Finally, Edison did not achieve his success alone – **network excellence** was an intrinsic component of his achievements. A large part of Edison's "genius" was his ability for what Professor Andrew Hargadon at the University of California calls a "technology broker," that is, the ability to connect and combine different facets of science and technology, through ideas and people, to solve a range of technical and practical challenges.[3] Perhaps nowhere was this more obvious than his creation of Menlo Park, an institution set up by Edison to generate a constant flow of technological innovation. At Menlo, Edison brought together people and technology to create an innovation engine that produced hundreds of new patents. Every scientist and engineer working at Menlo brought with them a web of connections that enabled them to further other people's work, often by pursuing new ideas and solutions across the traditional boundaries of electrical, mechanical and chemical engineering.

While Philo Farnsworth may have had "cognitive flexibility" and "strategic resilience" in spades, he lacked the networks and the social capital to bring his invention into the world successfully. And Philo is not alone. Too often "inventors," and we use this word in the broadest possible sense of people who generate new ideas or applications, succumb to the light bulb illusion themselves. In an interesting essay on a related theme called "The Televisionary," Malcolm Gladwell made an interesting point on this topic: too often we see large organizations as being contrary to the pursuit of invention and innovation.[4] However, in truth, when working effectively, organisations offer a range of benefits to the lone inventor: a network of people and expertise, the protection of intellectually property and the execution of basic administrative duties. In this sense, when invention happens, it is as much about context and connections as it is about bright ideas.

Andrew Hargadon, Professor of Entrepreneurship and Innovation at the University of California, argues that given the contrary nature of creativity itself, any would-be innovator needs to adopt complementary social strategies. Professor Hargadon has described creativity as a "chimera," something that is composed of two fundamentally different elements, each of which cannot exist without the other. So to be "creative" (that is to generate something novel) individuals need to break out of the world in which they exist, moving away from convention and dominant paradigms, in order to find new ways of perceiving, developing and expressing fresh ideas. Conversely, to enable those ideas to thrive, someone has to engage with the old world and find ways to embed new ideas by building new connections with people who will eventually find those ideas of real worth. We talked to Andrew to understand whether he believed that the person who develops the idea should also be the same person that entrenches the idea to help its survival.

> Should it be the same person? It's a tricky question and not one that should have a fixed answer. Broadly speaking, I think the answer is not necessarily so. My experience both in industry and academia suggests that most people are either good at one thing or the other, but not both.

Professor Hargadon's starting position prompted us to ask whether the "inventor" passes the baton to someone more commercial. "Look, that's a dangerous metaphor," he responded. "It implies a real separation between the two individuals: you know, someone comes up with a great idea and someone else turns it into a commercial proposition. In practice, it's just not like that. There is much more of a symbiotic partnership than the metaphor suggests. Think about Elvis Presley and his producer Sam Phillips. When they combined a popular country ballad, Blue Moon of Kentucky, with a Rhythm and Blues beat, they introduced the traditional sounds of R&B to a white teenage market that had little prior experience. That musical innovation depended on both of them working together. What people sometimes fail to recognize is that the commercial opportunity often shapes the creative output. Go back to

Edison. Originally, he had a 40W light bulb he could have tried to sell, but he recognized that the general public wanted something gentler in the home environment, so he went with the 13W bulb. It's a point that scientific entrepreneurs often miss; that is, the need to 'dial back the technology' to meet the market."

The point about the importance of the relationship directed us toward the importance of trust. We briefly explored this point with Andrew, who had this to say about the topic: "If this relationship is to work, then there has to be mutual respect, recognition of what each party brings to the situation. And trust is part of that equation. It might seem obvious, but in practice it often gets forgotten. A significant amount of energy and focus has to be invested in this sort of working relationship if it's to reap real benefits."

Professor Hargadon's work and focus has been on the irrefutably social nature of effective innovation. However, the collaboration does not end with a partnership between two people, or a team of individuals working on a common project. When creativity and innovation is really apparent, it can have a much broader influence.

INNOVATION, NETWORKS AND SOCIAL CAPITAL

Perhaps the most striking aspect of the skyline in Florence is the dome of Santa Maria del Fiore. It soars majestically and unforgettably above the waves of terracotta tiled roofs of the surrounding buildings. Built by Filippo Brunelleschi in the early part of the fifteenth century, it remains today the largest dome built of bricks and mortar in the world. The dome is not just a feat of great engineering, it is the result of an architectural design that valued the aesthetic as much as the practical. Csikszentmihalyi is an eminent psychologist who wrote an elegant book on the nature of creativity.[5] In it, he points out that Brunelleschi was not alone in producing outstanding works during this period. The first fifty years of this century proved to be an incredibly productive period – the "golden years" – for the Renaissance. Some of the most influential works of art were created in Florence during the same period. Aside from the dome, the bronze doors (the "Gates of Paradise") by Ghilberthi and the sculptures of Donnatello all represent works of art that are timeless artistic treasures that set the standard throughout the Renaissance period. Csikszentmihalyi also highlights that this bountiful period of the Renaissance raises an interesting question. Why was Florentine art so prominent during the Renaissance? It's a question that students and enthusiasts of the Renaissance period have been debating for over 600 years – and which goes to the heart of the light bulb illusion. It may seem like the inhabitants of fifteenth-century Florence just had more than their fair share of individual creativity. It may seem that the Florentine educational system somehow endowed their children with unusually gifted creative talents. The truth is that, while these artists were creative and talented in their respective fields, the opportunity to develop and demonstrate those talents was equally a question of context and connections. There are several factors which lay at the heart of this artistic explosion: The sponsorship and the patronage of the ruling families; a refreshed understanding of Roman building techniques; the tapestry of relationships between people at different levels of Florentine society; and the connections between the artists themselves. All of these factors contributed to the creation of a city with a unique set of social networks and a web of social capital that enabled individual talent to flourish.

And what was true in terms of creativity and innovation for Florence at the beginning of the Renaissance is still relevant today for any organization. To pursue this point, we interviewed someone who knows more than a little about innovation and creativity. Sir Christopher Evans is the founder and Chairman of Merlin Biosciences Limited. Founded in 1996, Merlin Biosciences manages or advises over €500 million and is one of Europe's largest venture capital firms specializing in life sciences. It invests in companies that are bringing to market human medicines or medical devices with groundbreaking technology and great commercial potential. He is regarded as one of Europe's leading biotechnology entrepreneurs having established over fifty companies and twenty successful flotations of high-quality science companies on five different Stock Exchanges. The businesses he has founded have achieved a combined value of €3 billion and employ 3,000 people. They have made substantial returns for their venture capital and institutional backers; of note is Chiroscience plc. that merged with Celltech plc. and was widely recognized as one of Europe's flagship bioscience enterprises companies until it was sold a few years ago.

We sat down with Sir Christopher and asked him what his thoughts are, in broad terms, about what makes organizations innovative. With characteristic straightforwardness, he set about keeping our conversation grounded and practical. "Look, first of all, let's be clear what you mean by the terminology." Defining our language was not a bad place to start: too often when discussing these topics with interested parties in previous workshops, or in researching this chapter, the words "improvement," "innovation" and "creativity" had been used interchangeably. This sometimes led to conversations becoming abstract and as a consequence, difficult to fathom the practical implications.

Let me tell you what I mean by "innovation." Innovation, at its most basic, is about changing things for the better. Now to achieve that end you might come up with a new drug, or cancer treatment; equally, you may well be talking about how you better tackle your customers, how you develop your best people or how you creatively market your products and the organisation. So let's be clear: innovation is not the exclusive domain of the R&D department. Innovation involves everyone and everything. But innovation by itself isn't enough. This is what a lot of organisations forget.

In addition to innovation you need "entrepreneurship." What do I mean by that? It's about the way in which you go about innovating in business. It involves doing things at pace, with clarity, taking sensible, calculated risks. People think that you can eradicate risk with a lot of careful planning and processes. You can't. If there isn't a small knot in your stomach when you are trying to do something new, the chances are it isn't. And that doesn't mean doing things alone or by yourself. Everyone needs some help to fill in the skills gap.

Take me, for instance. When I first started out in business, I was a scientist. I had a great range of new product ideas, but what did I know about business plans and finance? Nothing. And that's OK, by the way. It's OK to say that you don't know something or aren't good at something – as long as you get the help. That's what I did. I went to my old Professor, who I hadn't seen for while. I said to him, "I've got a great idea to start a business based on enzymes, but I don't know how to sort the finances out." He said, "no problem, Chris, go see a friend of mine. He picked up the phone and rang a contact and within a week or so, I was getting some of the best business advice in the world direct from a successful chemistry entrepreneur – and getting it free of charge! It's the same with marketing. I didn't know anything about marketing, but I knew someone who knew someone that did. I hired him and learned everything he knew.

And in the companies I've created, when you put "innovation" and "entrepreneurship" together, when those two things are truly part of the whole organisation, when everyone genuinely combines the innovation with the entrepreneurship and doesn't just talk about it, then you get real "enterprise" – an organisation that has real purpose, that goes about achieving that purpose with boldness.

Our interviewee's impromptu responses offer a practical view of innovation with several nuances. Firstly, Sir Christopher's definition of an "enterprise" is not limited to companies in the private sector. The attributes he described are important to any type of organization. Indeed, fifteenth-century Florence was clearly an enterprise – a place with tremendous clarity of purpose and daring. At a time when Western governments are propping up financial institutions with an unprecedented amount of public money, organizations in the public sector will face even more daunting challenges to deliver "more for less." This may be a burning platform to build enterprising public sector organizations as they have never been seen.

Secondly, he alludes to a characteristic of effective organizations that is often overlooked; namely, high performance contains an element of the "what" (that is, goals, objectives, KPI's, the necessary process steps, etc.) and the "how" (the behaviors that ultimately ensure that the "what" is achieved). From Sir Christopher's vantage point, the process and goals of innovation have to be combined with the "how," that is, those behaviors that constitute effective "entrepreneurship." Without entwining these two separate strands of organizational life, we run the risk of not realizing the potential of the people who inhabit those same organizations. What is also obvious during this interview is that constituents of the "what" and the "how" are relevant from the mailroom to the boardroom.

Finally, and most importantly for us, when talking about either the success of his organizations, or his career – all of which have taken place in a sector which is, by definition, innovative and entrepreneurial – it is clear that relationships really matter for Sir Christopher. In his early entrepreneurial steps, there is more than a quiet echo of Edison's ability to connect to other people to help him deliver his goals. In Chris' more recent career as Chairman of Merlin Biosciences, there is the obvious similarity in his ability to function as a technology broker. For us this underscores the point we have been making since Chapter 1.

When looking for the underlying reasons for success, the crucible of human interaction is essential. And when being entrepreneurial and innovative are the dominant facets of an organization, then that organization is likely to adopt the "enterprising" approach that Sir Christopher describes. We call that sort of organization a "collaborative enterprise" and to clarify what we mean by that term, let's turn to an unlikely source.

The corner of West Fayette and Monroe streets in Baltimore, USA has been made infamous far beyond the frayed edges of this inner-city neighborhood. The drug dealing and economic deprivation featured as the focus of a powerful book called *The Corner* by David Simon and Edward Burns.[6] Focusing on this narrow strip of urban life, and told from the perspective of a family fractured and broken by drugs, the authors told a universal story of crime and the slow burn decay of modern urban life. The book formed the basis of a television series called *The Wire*, which the critics in America raved about for its singular lack of sentimentality, for the demands it places on its audience to engage and think about the unfolding storyline and for a riveting depiction of real-life in the margins of American society.

The Corner describes in detail the workings of modern drug-related crime. It charts how the arrival of cocaine on the streets of America fundamentally changed the structured and neatly demarcated market created by heroin. Whereas gangs used to ply their trade within the confines of their own hard-fought "territories," the ubiquity of cocaine and its pharmacological derivatives enabled gangs to compete against each other on the same corners in a fierce form of retailing where the street perception of a specific product's "blast" value was the crucial factor. More than anything, cocaine made drug dealing a boundary-less crime. Cocaine created this boundaryless trade through ease of availability, simplicity of production and a shortening of the insidious supply chain from the crack head to dealer. This was no longer a serious drug manufactured by the few and consumed by a narrow range of hardcore consumers undeterred by subcutaneous infusion via syringe. This drug in all its different forms created a frenzied market that reached out across boundaries, both geographical and social.

The adaptive social networks of West Baltimore gangs and their booming but illicit industry have something to teach us in our context. Their distributed economic endeavor is essentially a collaborative enterprise. At its core, the collaborative enterprise is an organization without boundaries. Or at least its boundaries are permeable to new ideas, products and people. Traditionally, in the last one hundred years, our organizations have been created as commercial and physical edifices within which everything is planned and tightly controlled. Like the street gangs of old, they operated from and within fixed locations, offered a narrow range of products or services and used hierarchy as a means of communication and control. They were impossible to get into without the right combination of patronage, persuasion and apparent experience. In contrast, the collaborative organization does not operate according to these outmoded constraints. It succeeds through flattened, informal structures and reaches out to different markets by competing and then collaborating with competitors with a range of products, services and solutions. One of the most important characteristics of a collaborative organization is an uncertain sense of where the "inside" of the organization ends and the "outside" begins. And perhaps nowhere is this truer than in relation to the concept and practice of innovation.

A traditional view of innovation is that it occurs within organizational boundaries. In extreme circumstances, innovation only happens within the constraints of the R&D department of that organization. And, when in the thrall of the light bulb illusion, it happens only within the cranium of a single individual that occupies a desk in the darkest corner of the R&D department. That traditional notion of innovation has begun to wither – although it's far from gone – and in its place a more "open source" approach has started to become more apparent. In the purest sense, "open source" refers to computer software for which the source code is freely available. Its popularity and practicality has been fueled by the development of the Internet. More recently, "open source" has become synonymous with a form of mass collaboration on anything from the development of new code for Lego's sophisticated Mindstorm robots to the writing of collaborative novels online. This approach is neatly summed up and elaborated in a book called *Wikinomics* by Don Tapscott and Anthony Williams.[7] *Wikinomics* has become one of those ubiquitous business books that has managed to break out of its immediate market and gained itself a mass popularity. During the first few pages of their book, the authors offer a case study of open source innovation that captures its essence and the potential value to organizations.

This striking example centers upon Goldcorp. In the late nineties, this Toronto-based mining company had more than its fair share of problems: industrial action, significant debt and a gold mine that refused to yield up new gold deposits. Many analysts thought that Goldcorp's days were numbered. At the time, the young CEO Rob McEwen seemed unable to find a solution, but took some time out for personal reflection and development at an MIT conference for young Presidents.[8] It was when the conversation turned to Linux, an operation system developed and popularized though "open source" that he hit upon an idea that might save the company. Why not offer up all the geological data for the mine to the outside world and challenge someone on the outside of the organization to suggest the most likely location for new gold deposits. This was an idea not without its challenges. As Tapscott and Williams point out, the mining industry is notoriously clandestine and openness of the degree McEwen proposed did not come without resistance and suspicion. Nevertheless, in March of 2000, McEwen established the Goldcorp Challenge, which promised a total of $570,000 in prize money offered up to those individuals that proved to have the most accurate recommendations about locations of gold within the geological field. Tapscott and Williams report that the competition resulted in huge amounts of new gold being discovered; an outcome that helped the organization grow from a $100M company to a "$9 billion dollar juggernaut."

Goldcorp's strategy enabled it to become a collaborative enterprise that broke down its own organizational boundaries and succeeded where its previous inward-looking culture had failed. Every step of the Goldcorp journey is notable for the "bridging" required to generate new solutions. In 2006, McEwen had this to say about the success of his approach: "[Y]ou need to search for the unquestioned assumption in an industry and then question it. If you do that, you will shift your perspective and generate alternatives that people haven't thought of." No doubt the fact that McEwen came from outside the mining sector supported a clearer view of industry assumptions. It may also have helped in enabling him to make the analogous leap from Linux and open source to the collaborative analysis of the mining data.

Perhaps the "purest" form of collaborative enterprise can be found with an organization called Innocentive.[9] Essentially, Innocentive is an online market place where organizations with technical/innovation challenges can be brought together with experts from all round the world who may be able to offer solutions to those challenges. Innocentive began as a start-up through the e-division of Eli Lilly, a global pharmaceutical company, but has become an independent company in its own right. For a fee, Innocentive brings the organization (the "seekers") together with the people who might be able to offer help (the "solvers"). Currently, problems and challenges are broken down into a range of disciplines, from Chemistry to Global Health; from Food & Agriculture to Physics. Innocentive is a boundaryless world that has created an open innovation market place for an ever-growing range of companies and industries. The real question in our context is what are the implications for leaders and their leadership if they are to develop and sustain these innovative, collaborative organizations?

LEADERSHIP AND INNOVATION

Leadership is critical for innovation. Last year, McKinsey – the global strategic consulting organization – published some research which suggested that 65 percent of leaders were only "somewhat," "a little" or "not at all confident" about their ability to encourage innovation. This is a stark statistic given that 70 percent of leaders in the same survey assert that innovation will be one of the top-drivers for growth over the next five years. Of course, as soon as we start asking questions about the link between leadership and innovation, we become engaged in a debate about the relationship between the individual and their social/organizational context. So once again we stray into a zone of intellectual conflict where the fog of war occludes our vision. In 2006, at Wharton Business School at the University of Pennsylvania, the then Professor of Leadership and Change Management led a panel discussion titled: "Connecting the Dots Between Innovation and Leadership." The purpose of the debate was to define "exactly" how you put leadership and innovation together. Despite the very precise agenda for the forum, the conversations produced a conflated sack full of random thoughts that ranged from "there is no magic 'Aha!' moment – it's all just hard work" (the Wharton Finance Professor) to "you always have to reinvent yourself" (CEO of Deutsche Bank Americas) to "you need to be a differentiator in our industry" (CEO of MetLife). Rather than connecting the dots, the debate seemed to sprinkle the issue with clouds of new dots that further obscured the possibility of any answers.

During our interview with Andrew Hargadon, we asked him about the link between leadership and innovation. His responses offered some useful insights and more than a suggestion that McKinsey walks its own talk in this area.

"The main problem here is that organisationally the focus tends to be on individual performance rather than the performance of teams. If leaders are serious about innovation, they have to focus on networks and collaborative working rather than always scrutinise performance at the individual level. That's not easy to do, particularly as the performance appraisal systems for most organisations really target the individual. Leaders have to create organisational systems that enable people to develop those networks over time. This is where some of the better companies have got it right – they ensure their people move through functions, roles and geography so that when that person does take up a senior leadership role, they have a network that enables them to reach out to all parts of the organisation, no matter how big or how siloed.

We asked Andrew for any notable examples where organizations had achieved this focus on networks:

Well, McKinsey seem to have got this right. McKinsey evaluate your contribution to the firm not in terms of your technical knowledge, or just individual performance, but in terms of how you have come to know people across the organisation. It's not necessarily about having the right answer, but having the right connections to the people who may have the answer to the problem, or at least be able to help. And for McKinsey it doesn't stop there. McKinsey put in place a rapid response team that promised to connect you to someone else in the organisation who would be able to help with your client's problem within 24 hours. Those two aspects of the McKinsey organisation help to create a real focus on the importance of networks that will share and generate ideas.

McKinsey, in their quarterly journal, have talked about their own considered response to the issue of leadership and innovation. They propose a three-pronged approach that places a strong emphasis on networks and social capital. Their recommendations include (1) formally integrating innovation into the strategic plans of the organization; (2) creating the conditions for "dynamic networks" to develop and flourish across the organization; and (3) fostering a culture of trust among employees. To tackle the design of an innovative network, McKinsey offer a four-component model that illustrates key steps for leaders.[10] These revolve around connecting, setting boundaries and engaging, supporting, managing and tracking. The McKinsey model offers some straightforward advice at an organizational level, but it still falls short of clarifying what sort of leadership behaviors are needed to develop and support innovation networks within organizations. For example, in terms of building trust in the network, the McKinsey model emphasizes the importance of investing time to make this happen, but does not explain how leaders need to behave if they are to engender trust among people who are in those networks. Our own work indicates that the Network Leadership model has something to offer in this regard. Through the lens of the model, we would argue that the elements of cognitive flexibility, strategic resilience and network excellence have a crucial role to play in developing and sustaining innovation networks. As we pointed out earlier in this chapter, without all three facets of the network – Cognitive Flexibility, Strategic Resilience and Network Excellence – leaders are unlikely to turn great ideas to practical applications that are valued by others.

At the very end of the *Farnsworth Invention*, there is a brief and romantic scene (in an idealistic sense) during which Philo Farnsworth can be found in a bar at nine thirty in the morning. He has a drink of Seagrams on the rocks. It's July 16, 1969 and the crowd of people in the bar with him are glued to the TV screen watching Aldrin, Collins and Armstrong liftoff in Apollo 11 for their historic mission to the moon. We won't tell you what Philo is up to – we'll save that surprise for when you go to see the play. Just as the countdown from Houston reaches zero on the TV, the theater is suddenly plunged into blackness to signify the end of the play. The lights come up slowly and, as always happens at the end of an absorbing piece of theater, you gradually become aware of the audience and the world around you. It's at this point there is recognition of the real connection between the creative experience of theater, and a successful, innovative organization.

Andrew Upton, an Australian playwright and screenwriter once said in a documentary about the art of theater: "[W]hat the theatre asks of you is that you engage." Without that sense of engagement – from the audience, the actors and the crew – that creative experience is diminished.[11] From Upton's perspective, "without the audience, the play is nothing." It's easy to consider the audience to be the passive recipient of the theater company's creative art. But Paul Jamieson, actor and director of leadership development company called The Leadership Theatre also warns against succumbing to that illusion. In discussion with us he commented, "[T]he dynamic relationship between audience and the actors in the theatre, that subtle, invisible interplay between the audience and the actors is always the source of a great performance. That relationship will ensure that either the performance that lives on in the memories of actors and audience alike; or a it's a performance that at the audience forgets before they have left the auditorium."

From our view in the "stalls" the same is true for innovation and organizations in that it demands complete engagement, the full-throated participation of everyone. Without that commitment – at all levels and in all functions – great ideas may never happen; and even if they do happen, they are unlikely to deliver the concrete results of their abstract promises. If leaders want their organizations to be truly innovative, they have to create an ensemble experience for everyone – inside and outside the organization. No one is a passive bystander in the innovative organization: everyone, *collectively not individually*, has a contribution to make. This is the essence of the light bulb illusion – it requires an aptly balanced social network aligned and engaged to ensure the movement of concept through to completion. To achieve this, leaders have to keep themselves and their people continuously open to novel experiences, fresh perspectives and new faces. In short, to continuously innovate, organizations also have to continuously learn. So it is to the topic of development, and leadership development in particular, that we now turn to.

7

LEADERSHIP DEVELOPMENT: OF FIRES AND FORGES

Minds are not vessels to be filled, but fires to be fuelled.
(Plutarch, source unknown)

Don't be under any illusion; developing people is big business. It's tricky to get an exact size of the market in terms of Dollars, Pounds and Yuan, but it manages to sustain tens of thousands of human resource professionals, industrial/occupational psychologists, various forms of coaches, whole consultancies and entire business schools – some of them sprawling minicities. Confronted with that plethora of choice, it's easy to take the path of least resistance: choosing the well-known brands, buying development interventions through a single supplier that can deliver in terms of scale and scope; opting for sheep dip solutions that ignore the subtle nuances of individual learning needs; the list goes on. In the next few pages we've opted to discuss a few key areas of people and leadership development that we think are useful, but which should be used with eyes wide open and a hand firmly on the purse strings. Wherever possible, we have tended to focus on those areas that we believe may be particularly useful for the development of network leadership.

This has been a difficult chapter to write. As two people who plough their professional furrow in the field of leadership development, we may be too close to the subject matter. We do have something in our favor, though: a healthy skepticism that enables us to stand back and adopt, if not a truly objective view, then a perspective balanced by our own differing prejudices. One of those prejudices is we believe that the theory and practice of leadership development to be infused with an unhealthy amount of evangelical zeal, which may start the pulse racing, but actually occludes our vision about what is truly useful. Yet another professional prejudice is that development practitioners are notable for their cant and their hubris, rather than their substance. So we have tried to calibrate this chapter by including examples of the good, the bad and the ugly. Some of these examples are written with tongue-in-cheek, but they are all true. Finally, since leadership development is such a broad church, fragmented and fractured by schisms and sects, we have focused unapologetically on only a few areas of development that we believe to be useful for the practice of network leadership and the development of social capital. Some of the examples are drawn from our own experience, others from either the beneficiaries of development, or proponents and practitioners themselves.

Let's start this chapter properly with a story that takes us to the shores of Africa. Anchored off the coast of Nigeria on a large commercial vessel called *The Twilight Star*, Captain Jim Kitchener stood on deck smoking a cigarette, breathing in the humid night air. It was Tuesday, November 15, 2006, and for the next week Captain Kitchener and his crew would be laying pipes to a gas source on the mainland. It was one of those evenings – silent with the sort of temperate African weather that kept the ocean lapping gently against the hull – which made all the sacrifices of the job worthwhile: the long stretches away from home and family, the hard work, the inherently dangerous nature of the job. As Captain Kitchener turned to head to his cabin, he recognized the faint sound of an outboard motor buzzing gently in the night breeze. Instantly, from relaxed and meditative, Jim Kitchener's nervous system lit up, giving him a massive shot of adrenaline. He knew almost without doubt that that the sound of the outboard motor was an early warning of Nigerian pirates approaching his vessel.

The International Maritime Board (IMB) monitors the incidence of piracy globally and in 2007 declared the coast of Nigeria the most dangerous piracy hotspot in the world. Gone are the cutlasses and the muskets; the modern day pirates are armed with machetes, rifles and rocket launchers. For mariners such as Captain Kitchener, the danger is very real. He and his crew are unarmed and have only the passive drills advocated by their employers as a means of defense. It's a growing problem and it presents leaders such as Jim Kitchener with life or death decisions.

On this evening, Captain Kitchener sounded the alarm; he and the rest of the crew locked themselves into the securest cabins. Their hope was that these pirates would be pure opportunists, on board to rip off the mobile phones and the laptops, and then would depart with the minimum of fuss. On this occasion, it was not to be. The pirates found their way down to the cabins and began hammering at the doors with machetes. Jim Kitchener ordered his crew to leave the vessel: something easier said than done since the only exit was via the small portholes at the back of the cabin. Nevertheless, the entire crew, followed by their Captain, squeezed through the aperture, dropped 100 feet into the ocean below and swam to shore where they waited rescue.

Exactly ten days later, Jim Kitchener found himself in the bar of a leading European business school after a two-day dose of "leadership development." Over the two days he had endured psychological profiling, co-coaching (essentially constructive conversations that our story's protagonist described as "mutual masturbation") and an online business simulation during which he had to make decisions about whether to manufacture teddy bears or toy soldiers. Rather than being surrounded by pirates, he had been encircled, prodded and probed by psychologists who had observed his every movement over the last forty-eight hours. After a couple of beers, one of his colleagues turned to him and asked him if he found the program challenging and useful. His response was one of puzzlement:

> I'm struggling to make the connection. I can't see its relevance. Last week I'm on one of our vessels and pirates are attacking us; this week I'm at some sort of academic holiday camp. What we do when we're on board can't be put into one of these neat two-by-two models. This stuff may be OK if you're a corporate suit, but it doesn't work for me.

Leadership development experiences at business schools can be either a source of inspiration or desperation. This is clearly an example of the latter. It's a true story, although the names and places have been changed to save some blushes (Jim Kitchener, by the way, was a real person – an alleged "cardsharp" who went down with the Titanic!). All the elements of the story are accurate: a vessel besieged by pirates off the Nigerian coast, a captain making critical decisions that would have real-life and death implications for his crew; and a leadership program, sponsored by the human resources function, that appeared to tick all the right boxes to develop leadership capability but which only managed to elicit a sense of despair and irritation from the participants.

Although this is an extreme example, it is by no means untypical. Over the last twenty years, both of the authors have observed, directly or indirectly, leadership development activities where the implicit logic guiding the organization providing the service seemed to be "we are the experts" and "you need to listen." It's not just business schools who have been guilty of this: It's any organization that places more emphasis on what they believe to be right over the engagement of their participants. This practice ignores the irrefutable first principle of learning and development: people are not passive sponges that spontaneously and gratefully absorb the wisdom of others. When learning really happens, it's when they are emotionally and intellectually connected to the learning experience. There is no way that Jim Kitchener and his fellow seafarers were going to submit themselves to the leadership program that we described. It's not that the content was wrong or below standard, or the deliverers of the program poorly skilled and lacking expertise. It's just that it seemed irrelevant to their roles as leaders in the organization. They were not engaged by the format or the face validity of the workshop.

During his commencement speech at Stanford University in 2005, Steve Jobs, the CEO of Apple, made exactly the same point about his own development.[1] He talked about the well-known fact that he had been a college dropout; the courses just seemed too expensive and lacked the relevance to properly engage him. He then revealed is a lesser known fact about him: for the next eighteen months he became a "drop-in": Jobs stayed on campus, sleeping on the floors of friends' apartments and choosing courses that were just attractive to him. One of those courses happened to be about calligraphy. He acknowledged to the Stanford crowd that there was no obvious reason why he attended the course other than he was attracted to the aesthetics of calligraphy. He loved the course and it made a lasting impression. Years later, when designing the Mac, he insisted on including in the software design the functionality that would enable the user to choose a wide range of beautiful fonts. It was one of these early characteristics of the Mac that gave the computer its cult status and which was copied by competitors in later years. The point that Jobs was making to the Stanford graduates is that learners have to emotionally connect with whatever it is they are learning about. It's no different when developing leaders of organizations; they need to see the relevance and engage emotionally with the experience in order to derive real value.

The methods and techniques for leadership development discussed in this chapter have been chosen because they have been demonstrated to have real efficacy. But underlying the research and the mechanics is a need to engage leaders emotionally and intellectually in their own development in order to nourish that innate drive, to breathe fresh life into their motivation – in short, to "fuel the fire." We discuss both "diagnostic" approaches and "development interventions," but beware there is not clear demarcation between the two; sometimes just the process of discussing and highlighting someone's strengths and relative weaknesses is an intervention in itself that can bring about behavioral change and performance improvement. Whether diagnostic or development technique, we've tried to give a concise overview of each with the intended purpose of highlighting the pros and cons of each approach.

However, the topic of leadership development does not end with the selection of appropriate tools and techniques. Let's, for a second, return to Captain Jim Kitchener. Two days after they had been rescued and the pirates had retreated to the dark hole from which they had emerged, Captain Kitchener was then faced with the need to persuade his crew to jump back on board and sail the vessel back to the home port. After some cajoling – some subtle and some of a more direct nature – all of the crew agreed to return to the ship. Then something happened that almost resulted in what you would call a mutiny. The parent company wrote an e-mail to each member of the crew asking them to estimate, within forty-five minutes, what time they had popped through the porthole and dropped a significant distance into the Atlantic ocean. Why? Because, as the letter clearly indicated, their moment of departure from the vessel was also the moment when the company took the individual off the pay roll. Crazy, but true. (Although interesting, we subsequently heard that the same applied to the crew of the Titanic – much to their (or their dependents') dismay their wages were stopped from the "hour that the crew member entered the ocean"). In the case of the Twilight Star, it was resolved as being the administrative oversight of a junior clerk sitting in the safety of a little cubicle on dry land. Of course, the company continued to pay the crew. Nevertheless it had a big impact on morale, and it raises an important point about leadership development: it doesn't matter how effective a development technique may be in improving individual skills, if the organizational context is not supportive or consistent with the skills you have developed, the learning is likely to have little impact. It did not matter how effective a leader Captain Kitchener might be when it seemed for a short time that the organization itself did not care about its people. No amount of empathy or rhetoric or influence on his behalf would have resulted in the crew returning to their posts. There are far too many organizations that invest significant time and money in developing their people, but forget to develop or change the organization in tandem. The organization is the forge where the commitment and talent of leaders become wrought into a style that will have consequence and impact. Ignore that context, and the return on investment (ROI) for leadership development quickly drains away. Consequently the last third of this chapter will address the notion of organizational context and change to provide a more holistic view of the topic.

For us, the organizational context plays an important role in ensuring that development professionals avoid an extremist approach to their work. What do we mean by that? Well, broadly speaking, development specialists can be subdivided into "deficit divas" or "strength optimists." The deficit diva works to a "deficit model" of people development, that is, they evaluate what your strengths and weaknesses are, and concentrate on developing those weaknesses. In contrast, the strength optimists advocate that we ignore weaknesses and only aim to develop those capabilities in which you are already strong. Our view is that you work on the skills and abilities that you need in order to perform effectively in your context. In practical terms, this means that you prioritize development depending on that context, the end result being that development may encompass both strengths and weaknesses, as long as they are relevant to performance.

A final thought. When it comes to people development generally and leadership development particularly, there is always talk of measuring the impact of the training in order to understand the ROI. That's right and proper, and given a straightforward framework, it can be straightforward and useful to do. Careful and imaginative evaluation can give the organization and the individual clarity about where the training has had impact, and where either the development intervention can be improved or where the individual should invest more time and effort in order to achieve the necessary benefits. Indeed, Liz Bridge, Head of Learning Services at Cranfield School of Management spoke to us about the tripartite benefits of effective evaluation. She described these as follows:

- for the organization – understanding the real impact of the intervention upon organizational performance;

- for the participant – to embed and reinforce the value of their continuous learning; and
- for the development providers – not just the kudos of being able to demonstrate the ROI of their programs, but gaining a deeper insight into human learning and development.

However, evaluation of learning and development often makes one important assumption: that the person is right for the training and the training is right for the person. A consistent facet of our work with clients over the last twenty years is that insufficient time is invested in assessing and evaluating the individuals before embarking on some form of learning process. Careful assessment is time and money well spent. It provides an overall baseline of capability, enables the individual to have a clear view of the challenges ahead and allows the organization to allocate the appropriate level and type of learning initiative to the individual. Without the assessment, evaluation becomes something a nonsense; the results are obscured by an opaque view of the person's initial capability

LEADERSHIP DEVELOPMENT AND THE THREE LAYERS OF THE INVISIBLE

If you cut through the waffle and the complexities of the leadership development literature, it all boils down to two factors: the need to reflect, and the need to act. No more, no less. Reflection develops the self-awareness needed for learning and personal change, while action will shift that understanding from the abstract to the concrete. This is the biggest challenge for both the learner and the facilitator of that learning – making that difficult leap from merely talking about what has been learned to really walking that talk in a way that has demonstrable impact. To achieve that impact requires a double shift in commitment from the individual: the first shift is to a state of openness to new observations about themselves and their world, that brings an openness, insight and clarity into how leadership performance can be achieved; the second shift is all about the commitment from the individual to apply learning continuously back in the work place.

From a network leadership perspective, taking learning and turning it into valuable action is a major challenge since to do that effectively, the leader has to reflect on what we've called the "three layers of the invisible." These three layers are the strategic context; the leader's social capital and effective leadership behaviors. We have outlined each of these layers below, together with some of the observations and techniques that may be useful to consider and apply. These three layers all play a role in shaping and prioritizing the direction of leadership development, as well as the techniques chosen to develop the individual. Our experience is that each layer is tackled in exactly the order as described – a sort of learning onion working from the outside to the inside. This ensures that there is a clear and obvious thread from the strategic challenges facing leaders to the actual behaviors required to deliver against those challenges.

Layer 1: The strategic context

Understanding the strategic context is essential. The context dictates the organizational and leadership capabilities that will make the difference between success and failure for any sort of organization. Context also determines what Killing, Malnight and Keys from IMD business school in Switzerland have usefully described as the "must-win battles" – the essential activities on which leaders and their people need to focus.[2] Sometimes it is difficult for leaders to "see the woods for the trees," particularly during difficult times, when everything may seem critical for organizational success. But as Killing et al. point out, "lots of priorities are no priorities." Without a clear view of the factors that are fundamental to success, leaders often overstretch themselves (and their organizations), falling into managerial activities rather than keeping a strong leadership focus. Leaders have to use everything at their disposal to see those invisible lines of influence that shape and impact their organizations.

Clarity of these factors is mostly achieved by the quality of conversations a leader may have with those around him, but as Professor Andrew Kakabadse, Professor of International Management Development at Cranfield School of Management, points out, great conversations, particularly among members of the board, are hard to come by.[3] Professor Kakabadse's extensive research with senior teams all over the world have led him to two conclusions: (1) "the quality of interactions amongst members of the executive can enhance or damage the organisation"; and (2) "there is a high probability on most boards that there are issues that should be discussed, but which are too sensitive and as a result, operational/opportunity costs are experienced." Professor Kakabadse's research makes potentially disturbing reading for those of us that might assume that a great senior team is always a happy team. In one of his recent global studies, eighty-five percent of people interviewed at board level did not share a view of their organization's competitive advantage with their colleagues. Equally worrying is that approximately eighty-seven percent of board members did not understand or recognize the contribution of their board level peers.

However, Professor Kakabadse argues that effective boards should have a high degree of "essential difference." "A core activity of the senior team should be to disagree," argues Professor Kakabadse, "but it's the way that those conversations and disagreements take place which is important. All of those conversations and debates should take place within a framework of a shared view of the outcomes they want the organization to achieve." Professor Kakabadse's research explicitly demonstrates the importance of relationships for leaders and the people around them; though he stresses that the pattern of those relationships are different to those that occur between managers below the board. The team dynamics of the board will never be a form of "executive love-in," a closely bonded unit that speaks with one mind. Professor Kakabadse's work reminds us that's not the purpose of the senior "team." His work also asserts the importance of human interaction and takes us back to our core theme – the importance of social capital.

Layer 2: Social capital

As we discussed in Chapter 3, social capital is the invisible sum of the relationships we have with people. Healthy social capital can lead to a diversity of opinion, fresh ideas and a view of the world that extends beyond the limited vision of a purely egocentric position. The research and our own experiences of conversations with leaders underline the importance of relationships for achieving the right balance of social capital to deliver results. The problem is how do leaders see the pattern of those relationships and the quality of that social capital? That question leads to an even more fundamental issue: what do leaders need *to do* to ensure the right balance of social capital for any given context?

We spoke to Andrew Hargadon, Professor of Innovation at the University of California about how he helps executives tackle this challenge. "It's not easy and you have to start with helping the person to identify the three or four most important strategic goals. The next step – and to be honest, this is easier said than done – is to ask the individual to draw up an ideal ego network map that will include everyone who would be useful for delivering those goals. Subsequently, you ask the individual to draw up their current network and to carry out a simple gap analysis." Professor Hargadon's approach chimes with our own work, but it raises two fundamental questions: What is an "ego network map" and how to you create one?

To answer the first question, an "ego network map" is a term the cognoscenti use to describe a graphic depiction of a personal network that takes the individual concerned and places him or her at the center of that map. "Ego network map" may, like a clumsy term, be invoked by the technocrats to create barriers to a more general understanding, but the word ego does raise an important issue. The network map is derived from the perspective of the individual at the center of the network and as such is susceptible to the bias and subjectivity of that person. It is entirely likely that when trying to depict the quality of relationships with other people in our network, our personal feelings and a varying lack of awareness will create an asymmetric view of those relationships. However, our experience is that with sufficient coaching and the right sort of challenge, most leaders can at least identify where their own views of these relationships is utterly unilateral and open to bias.

Take a look at the network map below (Figure 7.1). This is a map drawn during conversations with the HR Director (HRD) of a FTSE 250 organization as part of a coaching process. His three key strategic goals at the time were: to benchmark HR practices with organizations outside of his sector; to develop broad cross-functional relationships with key managers not sitting on the board; to foster trust among all members of the executive board. The key for the map is below. What do you think may have been some of his possible development areas?

After drawing the map, and in the light of the core strategic challenges, the HRD came to three conclusions: firstly, he had too few valuable contacts outside the organization. Secondly, he tended only to trust those people that he saw frequently, which was a real challenge given that many of the managers with whom he was charged to develop relationships sat in offices all around the world. Thirdly, and this only became apparent after the conversation, although the people with whom he

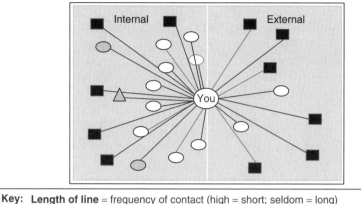

Key: **Length of line** = frequency of contact (high = short; seldom = long)
Shape = level of trust (square = low; oval = medium; triangle = high)
Colour = preceived value of relationship (black = low; grey = medium; white = high).

FIGURE 7.1 **Social network map – HR Director**

believed to have a high value, high trusting relationship (others members of the executive team), when they were questioned independently and privately, they had a very different view of the relationship. From just this simple exercise, this highly influential executive went back to the drawing aboard regarding how he sets about his key challenges.

While interviewing Professor Kakabadse, we asked him how he goes about tackling the dynamics of a senior team. "You have to begin with an assumption that each context is unique and that, as the outsider, your first job is to understand that context thoroughly. People often forget that – when looking at executive teams – what appears to be irrational and destructive behaviour – is often (when you understand their environment and their headaches) a perfectly rational response to a high pressure, challenging situation. Exploring how people think and feel with this independent view helps me to gain their trust but also enables me to retain a sense of impartiality." We then asked Andrew how, after interviewing people individually, he put this information together to help the team. "Before we get to the team dynamics, don't lose sight of the fact that these interviews form part of an iterative process. Also, I use psychological tools that help me to look at personality preferences, responses to conflict, etc. I contrast this information with what I draw from the interviews, then put it all together with the team to provide some candid, forthright feedback about the team's maturity and its capacity for handling change and delivering the organisation's strategic agenda. This process helps to raise awareness and build understanding and respect between each team member." One of the points that Professor Kakabadse is keen to emphasize is that he does not approach the team development process with a view to necessarily creating "harmony." From a network leadership perspective, the purpose of the executive team is more "bridging" to outside organizations and across functions than it is about "bonding" within the team.

Professor Kakabadse's work, and other similar interventions, hinge on the need to introduce someone external to the team and the organization to help develop the right balance of social capital. This may not always be the case, particularly if leaders demonstrate a keen awareness of their team dynamics and their own behavior. One of our more detailed case studies, Peter Lidstone, the Global Supply Chain Director for industrial giant Akzonobel Decorative Paints, revealed how this happened in relation to his own team. Peter's story is also a great example of how leaders need to shift the balance from bonding to bridging (or vice versa) as circumstances change. The following conversation also reveals how the simple process of drawing the network's evolution embeds learning and reveals new opportunities to develop them further.

The prompt for our interview conversation was the 2×2 matrix around Bonding and Bridging that we outlined in Chapter 3. We asked him to use the matrix as a lens to talk about his own development. Being an inveterate storyteller, he took up the challenge with gusto:

> When I moved into this role, the team I inherited was in disarray. My immediate goals and objectives were therefore crystal clear. Restore service, rebuild the team, address costs and improve efficiency. All of which could only be achieved through a tight focus on each member of the team and how they fit together. I needed to establish complete control in the short-term and could only do this through direct connections with everyone.

(Peter spontaneously illustrated what he meant with the diagrams below (see Figures 7.2a, b, c and d))

> That was my focal point and everybody knew what I was doing. I deliberately looked inward to the team and focused all of my energy on building those relationships. I set aside time with each

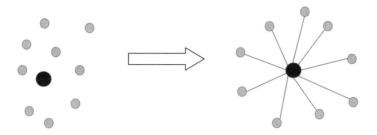

FIGURE 7.2a **Forming bonds within the team**

member of the team, explaining my priorities, direction and sense of how I wanted the team to look and work going forward. At the same time I was learning about their individual strengths and development areas, experience and aspirations. This took real time and commitment on my part – gradually working towards a shared sense of team stability and identity. I received clear feedback from my team that I had provided them with a higher level of certainty, having taken away much of the ambiguity and chaos that had distracted and frustrated them previously."

Having built a strong team, and realised some of those initial, critical benefits of having that team connected through me, it became increasingly obvious that this nevertheless had its own drawbacks. I became a hub – and no communication could occur without passing directly through me. Bob would come to talk to me about something that clearly he should be talking directly to George about. I realised at this stage then that I needed to add a "rim" to the team, and some interconnections, so that they could connect to each other directly, without passing through me.

So that was my next task. Building connections within the team that allowed them, in many instances to by-pass me. I could only do this once I had developed trust and effectiveness in the individual team members – but then I had to do it to free up my time to take the next steps. I now have less contact with individual team members, but still maintain very regular contact with the team as a whole. I have placed the emphasis upon meetings being their team meetings – that I frequently attend. Having established control I am now able to give it back to them. I am a participant, not an ever-present Chair. It has made a huge difference to their confidence, trust and team morale.

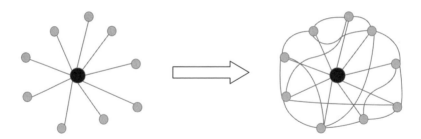

FIGURE 7.2b **Forging connections across the team**

The most critical next step after rebuilding the team was to start to connect myself (and later the team) to other teams and functions outside of our own.

We then asked Peter how he decided which alliances to prioritize?

To be honest that's pretty easy once you have been in a role for a while. You start to identify who are your potential allies. In my case the immediate targets were within Sales, Marketing and Finance. These are functions and groups that I have to talk to – directly – not just to share information – but to develop the way forward together.

The changes that we implement at this level are multi-dimensional and it is important to realise that everything we do is inter-connected. A decision that I make has a direct knock-on effect to many others. If we don't really engage at the beginning – as an interconnected team – there is a real risk that we are all going to pull in different directions without realising it.

So, I consciously set out to build my relationships with my counterparts in those other functions. That's not to say that they weren't there already to some extent – but there was consider-able scope to establish higher levels of trust, shared purpose and understanding of how we mutually impact and support each other.

At this point, the obvious question was how has this impacted the way Peter delivers his role?

[P]ut one way, you could say that increasingly I am doing almost no work. The majority of my time is spent in meetings, events and

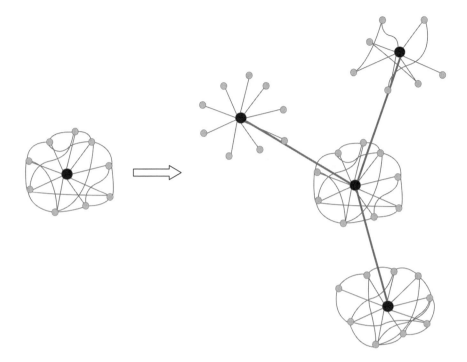

FIGURE 7.2c **Building bridges**

debates. Absorbing stuff, assuring, suggesting and challenging. This is about instantaneous communication – reacting and responding as much as planning and delivering. And it's with an ever-increasing and expanding set of people. It can be relentless. I have learned new ways of capturing actions and firing communication in the relevant directions. My old system of notebooks and lists simply doesn't work anymore. I have to type notes during or immediately after meetings and make sure that I action them before the next. Communication in this highly networked structure of relationships can't wait. The closer we can get to constant and open sharing of thoughts and ideas, as well as information, the more competitive we can be. And that benefits us all.

The story of relationships and social capital that Peter related showed how the nature of social capital shifts over time. We wondered whether this shift from bonding to bridging was "final":

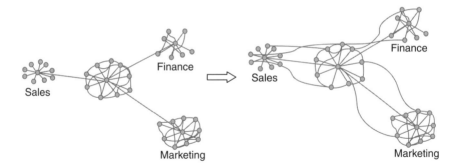

FIGURE 7.2d **Bridging and Bonding**

Definitely not! That top right hand box – the one that represents Bonding and Bridging is where I am, or at least am trying to be, right now. Not just connecting myself to these other groups and functions – but starting to connect them directly into my team. Because I need to get the balance right through all this. Remaining sufficiently close and supportive to my team, but also expanding their relationships and opportunities to share ideas and work across functions. Essentially, to stop myself becoming a different sort of hub all over again.

I hadn't consciously thought of it this way before. It's only when I draw this that I realise exactly how this has evolved – fascinating. But now that I have – it immediately prompts me to think of where I have opportunities to connect new people into my team; which new areas I can focus on for myself; and how I have to do all of this without neglecting my own core team.

Layer 3: Thoughts and behaviors

Our previous case study makes a clear case for looking at the behaviors we exhibit in the process of developing our social capital. In our final "layer of the invisible" the question then becomes: how do we know what sort of behaviors and how do we know the extent to which we are effective at demonstrating those behaviors? This is a fundamental question for a leader's development. To tackle that question, we are going to focus in this section on the use of 360° feedback as a tool that can really raise awareness and clarify development challenges for a leader before moving on to the use of coaching as a technique to take that awareness and drive behavioral change.

For the uninitiated, 360° feedback is the process of eliciting the views and comments from you and from the people with whom you work in order to identify behavioral strengths and development areas. Typically, the people that would be asked to participate in a 360° process would include your boss, your peers, the members of your team and possibly your customers. The questions are usually structured around the behaviors that an organization has found to play an important role in high performance. These questions can be asked face-to-face, but where this technique is used on a wide scale, they are typically presented online across either the company intranet or the Internet. This is a fast and efficient method to deliver this development technique to all the managers in your organization. Organizations may ask for responses to those questions in both qualitative and quantitative form.

Once everyone has completed the questionnaire, a report is generated which summarizes the quantitative data in simple bar charts that enable the individual to compare and contrast the feedback from different clusters of people. Some organizations insist that a third party is used to help interpret the results; others just send out the report and expect the recipient to fend for themselves. There are a number of huge benefits to be derived from such feedback:

- You see how people view your behavior from different perspectives. This is useful if you focus on picking up the patterns and trends, or any sudden reversal to those trends.
- Greater objectivity – based upon observations built up over time. The views captured about your behavior are developed over time with people, therefore it is less likely to be a "snap shot" of your capabilities.
- It is specific – looking at actual behavior rather than just personality. This is critical – professionally designed 360° questionnaires rely on clear behavioral statements that leaders can then focus on to enhance their own performance.

However, there are some pitfalls with the use of the 360° tools that need to be pointed out. Given the broad nature of this book, there is only a small space to outline some of the most important. To begin with there can be a massive "so what" factor with 360° reports; it can all just appear to the recipient of the feedback to be a pile of numbers that signify nothing. A fundamental principle therefore is to contextualize the feedback by spending time understanding the strategic context. This then enables the individual, either alone or in conjunction with a third party, to interpret what is really important from the feedback and to ignore the "noise." A second problem, and this usually happens when the person receiving the feedback is allowed to interpret the results alone without any help, is that there is an over-the-top focus on the negative. Typically, someone will take in their report, dwell for a short time on the positive feedback and seek out the low scores and critical comments, spending a disproportionate amount of time on the latter rather than the former. This is why it is so important for people to have either some training in the interpretation of the 360° report or a third party present to ensure the individual takes a structured, balanced and positive approach. This leads us to the third and final issue, and which is more "pratfall" than "pitfall" in our experience; sometimes individuals succumb to an overwhelming need to focus on the numbers in the report rather than strive to understand what the numbers mean. This then leads to the "mine is bigger than yours" conversations which, in one extreme situation at the UK headquarters of a certain investment bank, resulted in senior members of the organization engaging in scores that had been taken to three decimal places! On the whole, though, used with care and consideration, the 360° feedback process is potentially a hugely valuable tool in helping leaders to understand where to focus.

Our own recent use of 360° feedback has hinged on our model of network leadership that we discussed in Chapter 5. We have developed and used this tool both on a one-to-one basis and with small groups. In general, our use of this tool has led to three general conclusions:

- Feedback from a range of people on specific behaviors enables the individual to reflect clearly on what needs to be done to develop social capital that is "fit for purpose" in their context. It is also useful to break down exactly what sort of behaviors are relevant in order to dispel the myth that developing effective networks is all about "selling oneself." When it is at its most valuable is when it serves as a mirror to hold up to less self-aware individuals who may have no idea how their behavior is perceived by others.

- Critically, it has also demonstrated that the network behaviors specifically (and refer to Chapter 5 for a broad summary) are more useful when combined with the two other elements of network leadership, that is, cognitive flexibility and strategic resilience. Our experience here, we believe, underlines once again how understanding the whole context is essential for developing leadership capability.
- Lastly, we always use this tool in conjunction with social capital mapping exercises so that individuals are able to reflect on perceived behavioral patterns, the nature of personal networks and the quality of relationships within those networks.

To sum up this section, the development of network leadership requires the leader to focus on three areas that are not obvious to the human eye: the strategic context, the quality of their social capital and the consequences and impact of their day-to-day behavior. Over the last few years we have used all the techniques we have described to make the three layers of the invisible clear to the naked eye and so available for reflection and awareness building. We have also tended to approach those development activities in that same order, starting from the external world and moving to the internal environment – it's a more meaningful process and ensures that development stays focused on results. Now the question becomes, how does the individual move from awareness to action, from reflection to taking personal responsibility for making those actions happen? To tackle this theme – the second shift for personal development – we want to focus on one of the more popular tools currently for leadership development: coaching, but we will also give brief coverage to an innovative workshop design that has proved to develop these skills.

THE COACHING CONUNDRUM

We have opted to include the topic of coaching to address the second shift of personal development for a number of reasons. Firstly, its popularity has increased exponentially in the last five to ten years. Secondly, it is a disparate profession that often seems to lack coherence and discipline. Lastly, because when coaching is really effective it enables the individual to make that leap from reflection to positive action, even when operating in an organization where the structure, the politics and the people may seem less than ideal. To start, here are three vignettes that are all true stories.

Story one: Bad therapy

Graham Simmons (an entirely fictional name made up for the purpose of recounting this short story) stepped into the office to meet with the firm's organizational psychologist. The topic of the conversation: Graham's development as a leader, as a senior executive within this global organization. Graham was new to the organization and had come in as a general manager for a key business unit. The psychologist spent some time going over his career, the challenges ahead and the sort of development Graham had found useful in the past. The overall purpose of this conversation was to set up a stretching development plan for the next twelve months. When the conversation arrived at the point of deciding what sort of development intervention would be useful for Graham, he had already decided long before the meeting begun. He told the psychologist he wanted an "executive coach."

"Have you had an executive coach previously, Graham?" The psychologist asked.

"Indeed," said Graham. It was possibly the most useful development experience I've ever received."

"That's great, Graham. How long did you work with your coach?"

"Oh, about five years. We've not really stopped. I paid for some of the recent sessions myself."

The psychologist took a breath before responding:

"Graham, that's not coaching – it's therapy. And bad therapy at that."

Story two: The manager bypass

The vice-president for sales sat down opposite the HR Director with a fixed smile. He had a problem and a plan to resolve the problem, but he wasn't sure the new HR guy would see his solution in the same terms.

"My previous CEO always said come with solutions, not the problems." This was the VP's opening gambit: the "relax, don't worry,

I've got this under control, just sign off the expenditure" approach. The Group HR Director just smiled and said nothing. The VP ploughed on:

"Simon is a bit of a problem, but fundamentally, he's a good guy. He hasn't been performing for the last six months and I know he pissed off the customer last week, but he's a solid performer normally."

The HR Director continued smiling, but still said nothing. This was becoming a bit irritating.

"I've had some chats with him and I know what he needs to really get him back on an even keel … I really get the point about his poor relationships with the manufacturing guys."

Silence.

"Look, he just needs a coach."

Story Three: Who's coaching whom?

This was Kirk's first meeting with his new coach. It was part of some new development scheme the HR department was pushing. The coach seemed to have a great CV – although Kirk wasn't sure what a great CV for a coach really looked like. The phone on his desk rang. It was reception: his coach had arrived!

"Sit down. Sorry about the cramped conditions, but it was the only office free for our meeting other than mine – and I thought it best not to meet there." Kirk sat down next to Allison Priestly, executive coach. He was feeling a little nervous by the process, but wanted to make sure his coach felt really relaxed and able to do her thing. Whatever "her thing" might be.

"Thank you, Kirk. I love this space. We don't need a table. It's a very intimate room – exactly right for the coaching experience." Allison explained.

For the next fifteen minutes Allison carefully deconstructed Kirk's role, his contribution to the organization and the extent to which he was happy with his life more generally.

"Broadly speaking, I'd say everything is going great for me … just been promoted, had our second child, so besides a lack of sleep I'm very happy." Kirk explained. He looked across at Allison. She said nothing. Her head was in her hands.

"I wish I could say that about my life," she responded.

"I beg your pardon," Kirk was a bit surprised about her response. Perhaps it was all about the coaching process – mutual self-disclosure or something.

"No, really. I'm having a terrible day. I just can't deal with one of my business partners." Allison started to cry.

"Hey … don't cry," said Kirk, "I'll make us some tea and you can tell me all about it."

The stories are all true. Compressed by time and the need for brevity, they are somewhat exaggerated, but they are still an accurate representation of situations of which we have been aware in the last twelve months. We have started with these three vignettes, not because we think that coaching is not a worthwhile tool to develop people – it is; but because the combination of the meteoric rise in the uptake in coaching, together with a lack of rigor and professionalism among certain facets of the coaching community, have created a raft of new problems. So rather than starting with an evangelical view of the value of coaching, we want to point out some of the possible bear traps.

In the first example, coaching has become a psychological crutch for the manager. Dependency is always a potential pitfall in coaching, but this seemed to be an extreme example where someone had been exploited with no obvious benefit other than the fees paid to the coach. For the VP in the second vignette, coaching represents a way to bypass management responsibilities. He no longer has to manage the individual concerned, or take any tough decisions about the individual. The coach has taken on the dirty work for him. And, finally, the third story reveals both the misunderstanding about what people expect from the coaching process as well as the inappropriate behavior of the coaches themselves.

This may seem a little unfair to the coaching fraternity. It is. But it does not move us away from the fact that coaching has to get its act together. To explore where the profession might be going, we talked to a number of people in the coaching profession who have reputations for professionalism and delivering results. One of the people we interviewed and who seemed to talk a lot of sense was Jez Cartwright, CEO of a specialist coaching company, "Performance Consultants."[4]

We met Jez Cartwright at an annual HR conference that takes place on a cruise liner that sets sail from Southampton and which drops anchor off the coast of Guernsey for a couple of days, trapping a sizeable population of senior HR professionals with an array of enthusiastic suppliers, ranging from the usual sharks to an engaging babble of interesting individuals who have something useful to say. Fortunately for us, Jez is at the latter end of that continuum. We asked him his view of coaching as a profession.

It still remains very much an emerging market. Way beyond the buzzword it used to be. Some of what has happened around coaching is good, some of it considerably less so. Many of those people practising as coaches have not had any training in coaching, and often have not had any professional development themselves. It's people at this end of the profession who can completely screw the reputation of coaching for others. The field attracts an incredibly wide range of people from psychologists to counsellors, from niche therapists to business consultants: all of them *seizing the opportunity* to operate under the banner of coaching.

We asked Jez to do something we have asked many other people to do: define coaching in simple and straightforward terms.

At its most elemental, it's about helping the individual to help themselves. Coaching has to be very flexible, but essentially it has two components: (a) identifying the issue and (b) making sure the individual makes some progress in relation to that issue. The role of the coach is to support the individual through that process. Sometimes, it's an easy run – you work with someone who recognises the need and works hard with you to improve performance. Frequently, though, you might have to work with people who pay lip service to improving performance and need to be pushed very hard to the point of improvement – even if there is a little kicking and screaming on the way there. I believe that coaches have to work in partnership with the individual and the organisation. It's vital for the success of the process that you help both the individual and the organisation to develop a contract, albeit informal at times, about what success looks like for the coaching process. It's interesting, sometimes organisations appear to be a bit reticent to becoming involved in defining outcomes. But for me, it's not optional. There has to be a shared sense between the organisation, the individual and the coach of what constitutes a successful return on investment.

As Jez raised the issue of qualifications and relevant experience, we pressed him about his own qualifications:

I have a Masters in the Science of Sports Coaching. My initial experience focused on coaching elite sports' teams: the England cricket team, diving and rowing teams and various premier football teams. I then took a CEO course in coaching and eventually moved into executive performance coaching. But let me declare my hand here. I do think that qualifications and formal education are important; but they shouldn't create a slavish adherence to process. Great coaching can often be results focused and structured, but it shouldn't suffocate the creativity and the energy of the person you are coaching. When you get the balance right, the results can be remarkable.

In discussing coaching with experts like Jez Cartwright, we seemed to arrive at a partial confirmation of our own experience: that coaching is successful when it's done properly because it helps to contextualize learning. The coaching dialogue enables the developing leader to retain motivation, of course, but it also enables him or her to plot a course through the politics and processes of their own organization, which really helps to embed their insights, change behavior and improve performance. It is this acknowledgment and sensitivity to the context, and the relationships in that context, that make coaching such a great vehicle for developing network leadership.

There are some intrinsic problems for an approach to developing leadership that is solely based on coaching: it is resource hungry, potentially expensive and, consequently, it is aimed typically at a narrow range of individuals. There are complementary alternatives that have demonstrated their worth and which can reach a wider audience with less cost per head. Ron Burt, the impassioned professor of social networks at Chicago Business School carried out a careful study that demonstrated how an executive education program for groups can have positive consequences for networks, performance and career development.[5]

The program took place at the Chicago Booth School of Business and was designed for Raytheon, one of America's leading technology companies. The goal of the program was to teach executives about the network structures underlying different facets of social capital in order to build a leadership cadre that would be more closely aligned with strategic initiatives and could operate across divisional boundaries within Raytheon. Burt's program lasted five days and used a range of techniques: "chalk and talk," case studies, DVD's and participative exercises. There were mandatory projects that enabled the individuals to apply the principles they had learned, and follow up sessions at various points after the program.

The results of the program are impressive. Relative to a control group of untrained but otherwise similar colleagues, the research team made the following conclusions about executives who went through the program. The participants were

- 36–42 percent more likely to receive top performance ratings.
- 43–72 percent more likely to be promoted.
- 42–74 percent more likely to be retained by the organization.

Let's put aside the last piece of evidence: employees who go through such programs often develop a favorable impression of the organization that enhances retention, and this will have little to do with the actual content of the program. Nevertheless, the results are impressive. It provides hard data – which although needing some debate and discussion – suggests that there are aspects of network leadership that can be taught in groups.

Given that part of our argument in this chapter is about the intrinsic importance of motivation in the development process, Professor Burt and his colleagues revealed another important aspect of their study. Participants in the program who were viewed to be engaged and have an active participation in the program were later found to have benefited more significantly in terms of performance and career development than colleagues who had been deemed to be "passive." This is not a groundbreaking discovery: first year undergraduate psychology students know that active use of new information enhances learning more effectively than pure rote rehearsal. The real question here is what elicited the engagement? There are a host of possible factors. Burt argues that teaching the network structure of social capital represents an incremental addition to the executive education agenda. That may be true. However, it's also true that the program used a range of learning techniques which would have facilitated engagement of many of the participants. Whatever the reason, the message is clear: developing leaders has to be meaningful in order to deliver results.

The last section of this chapter has taken a selective stroll through some of the techniques that may be useful to develop network leadership skills. We've been ruthless with what we have included since this is potentially the subject matter for a whole book rather than the lion's share of a single chapter. Whether we've succeeded or not, we have tried not to take a rose-tinted view of developing people, highlighting some of the problems and the issues when organizations and individuals embark on a course of leadership development. Some of those problems are generic to the area; others are specific to our own views of leadership in particular. There is still one aspect of people and leadership generally we would like to discuss, and which is highlighted at the beginning of this book: the importance of organizational context. Consequently, the next brief section elaborates on this theme and offers some general thoughts about the importance of organizational design and development, alongside skills improvement at an individual level.

FROM FIRES TO FORGES

To begin the final few pages of this chapter, we offer you a personal story that illustrates the core of the dilemma. In the early part of 2009, we ran a second workshop on the topic of project management as part of a series of workshops intended to provide a general skills uplift for everyone involved in project management across the organization. The workshop had twelve delegates, all of whom had considerable project management experience, but none of whom had received much of what would constitute formal training. We found an external organization to deliver the workshops: two experienced guys with great project management experience and a terrific eye for designing engaging workshops. At the end of the workshop, we distributed the evaluation sheets ("happy sheets"), and sure enough the workshop had been well received, the scores on all factors coming out at 4's or 5's out of 5.

The next step of the development program was a specific project that each person had identified and which would be used as the framework for applying the principles learned over the last couple of days. We recall a bucket load of enthusiasm in the room and a real determination to get on and try new techniques, and for people to push themselves to raise the quality of what they were doing. There also seemed to be a greater enthusiasm for the organization generally. To be honest, we had a sense of real job satisfaction. We believed the follow-up workshop, planned for eight weeks' time, and during which the delegates would present back to us on what they had done to apply their learning, would help the organization to track progress but also give all the delegates the opportunity to showcase what they had been doing. We walked out of the training center to the sound of competitive banter behind us.

The eight weeks flew past. We all met again, this time with one of the executive team members present; he was there to listen to the various progress reports and to give a real sense that the organization considered learning and development to be a strategic priority. We looked around the room and saw none of the enthusiasm that we had observed at the end of the workshop. At the time we put it down to pre-presentation nerves. As the presentations unfolded over the next couple of hours, it was clear that presentation nerves was the least of our problems: most of the projects were incomplete, there was very little evidence of applied learning and instead of energized project managers, we were faced with the sort of laissez-faire demeanor that we had encountered before the workshops began. To say it was a disappointment is a significant understatement.

What had gone wrong? We spent several days interrogating each other, the staff, the external suppliers, the line managers of all the delegates. We checked that something significant had not occurred in the business units in which the project managers resided. We examined the pre-assessment reports for each person to make sure we had the right people in the room. We can recall pouring over the program detail, debating whether the content had been too abstract; or the examples too prosaic; the exercises too tangential; or whether the trainers had pulled the old wool over our eyes, and that they were not of the quality we had once imagined.

The sum total of this beaded scrutiny: nothing. We could not see how the program could have been improved, or how the delegates could have been of a better quality. When they had returned to their divisions, their workloads had been of a similar level to that which they had faced before the workshop: tough but not impossible. It took us days to wake up to the problem that had been staring at us in the face – nothing had changed. The project managers went back to work in the same teams, with the same line managers, within the same structures, with the same process tools, on the same projects. And in the middle of all this "sameness," the project managers were surrounded by a sea of people that had not been through the training, who didn't see that there was scope to improve, who had not reignited their passion for their work, who wanted to plod down the same well-worn groove that had become, to be honest, comfortably familiar. We had spent all our time focused on the structure of the learning and development; and very little or no time on the organizational structure, the context, in which the project managers were embedded.

Having finally come to the recognition that "development" in this case was more than a general skills uplift, we engaged the HR Director to seek his views. He saw the problem in an instant: we had assumed too much about the current organizational structure and the extent to which it was fit for purpose. He instantly set about a robust debate with other members of the board: the Group Operations' Director, the Sales Director, all four of the divisional directors and the CEO. After some frank exchanges of viewpoint, the CEO commissioned the Group Operations' Director to review the entire approach to project management and to come up with a proposal that would drive measurable performance improvements. Six months' later, the work is well underway.

We talked to Peter Scraton, Group HR Director of e2v – a global hi-tech manufacturing firm, about his thoughts on a similar experience:

It's a common mistake. People forget that OD and L&D are inextricably linked. Let me tell you about our organisation and how that connection has been utterly intrinsic to what we're trying to achieve as a business. For any company to thrive we need real diversity of people – with different skills, approaches and backgrounds. Historically we had what I would call a "monotone" legacy – technically strong people but often not sufficiently broad or equipped for the full range of roles that a large organisation needs to succeed in these very challenging times. One of our fundamental changes has been from a "Technical push" to a "Commercial pull." We have had to consciously redress this balance in our sales team for example. Similarly – a stronger emphasis upon Supply Chain focus rather than simply our own technical processes. Some of this has been through recruitment – but it is set in the context of the right structural context and the right people development.

What have we done in terms of organizational development? In e2v we have moved to a matrix structure in order to best deliver our challenging growth targets and thrive in an increasingly competitive landscape. The previous vertical integration structure was fit for purpose when the business was smaller and more tangible in terms of geography, products and market. However, as we have expanded (rapidly through M&A) the matrix approach is considerably more fit for purpose because it allows for the global scale in which we now operate. Through this structure – Divisions with devolved P&L – we can empower our senior leaders to resource and drive growth in a more accountable way; whilst our functional areas can leverage economies of scale and drive synergies across the Divisions.

But in the context that we're talking about now, this structure helps to change some critical behaviours in our leaders and staff. It forces them to work more closely together – to be aware of each others' roles, perspective and value. Previously, the level of trust between our Operations and Sales functions was low. Sales would put forward a forecast, but Operations would produce considerably less than needed – they fundamentally did not believe in the accuracy of the figures. This had a very negative impact upon delivery and customer satisfaction. The new structure, where these people share targets (through Divisional P&L), meeting space and are often geographically co-located, has significantly reduced tension and friction and increased trust and understanding. A similar benefit has been seen on product design – through Designers and Operations working more closely together. In my view, it is only when you get the right structure, that you can implement people development initiatives that can take hold and deliver obvious impact. The problem you described with the project management programme is not uncommon. It just requires more joined-up thinking.

This is not the place for a long discussion about the art and science of organizational design and development. Approaches to this field are many and varied, and it is beyond the remit of this book to unravel those varying methods and debate their relative importance to people and leadership development. Our intention here is only to assert, once again, the importance of context. We want to sound an alarm bell that alerts you to the possibility that an organization's focus becomes overtly and inappropriately concentrated on the individual. It's easy to do. We become blind to the wider impact of the context both because of complexity and because these factors are less obvious to the eye.

At its core, network leadership is about taking advantage of informal social structures, which will inevitably be shaped by the formal structures that govern and constrain day-to-day behavior. Like the Bank Wiring room studies in Chapter 4, the informal connections between people can often have unexpected consequence as a result of poorly considered organizational design. Consequently, leadership development (and not just for what we regard to be network leadership) should also encompass the principles and practices of organizational design. We should educate our leaders about how formal organizational structure is likely to make their roles as leaders either easier or considerably harder. The personal fire and sometimes fury of the individual leader is not enough to deliver real change for organizations. Organizations are the forges that provide the real heat to make leaders and managers malleable, ensuring that leadership development will have a sustainable and lasting impact.

8

ELEPHANTS, MOONS AND MIRRORS

In a very real sense, everything we see is an illusion. Some of those illusions are man-made, while others are naturally occurring. When we look at an object, light bounces off it and produces two-dimensional, inverted images on our retina, which then travel along the optic nerve to the brain where they become a three-dimensional, "right way up picture" in our mind's eye. To achieve that transformation, our brain interprets the data and the image we eventually perceive is a function of context, memory, genetics and motivations. Writing this book has been something akin to the process of human visual perception, although much slower! We started three years ago with some raw data – the basic idea and a book title. Our journey from the first meeting with the editor ("the basic premise is good, but the title is boring") to the last conversation with a friend about the final chapter ("don't make it too long"), has transformed that data into a richer, more colorful, and perhaps more useful interpretation than we envisaged at the beginning of our project. It has been a process that has confirmed a few things we believed, but has also highlighted a lot that we needed to consider and include. Our workshops and the in-depth interviews with leaders and their followers, academics and consultants, have provided the sort of reality and insight that have shaped and clarified the empirical (but sometimes opaque) perspective we had when first putting our fingers to keyboard. Of equal importance to the changing shape of this book and particularly this concluding chapter, is the radically different socio-economic climate in the aftermath of the recent financial crisis and our current economic recession. In a very real sense, this book has walked its own talk, highlighting the importance of "context and connections."

One of the areas where our ideas have evolved is in relation to the importance of the behaviors that create and sustain vibrant networks – the very heart of our argument. Take a look at the cover of the book. The two dominant features of the picture are the herd of elephants and the low-slung moon over the African horizon. The choice of both is no coincidence. The African elephant is an extremely social animal. For anyone lucky enough to have had the opportunity to observe these amazing and graceful creatures for any time in the wild, their patterns of behavior are fascinating to watch. From the sway of the trunk to the slow flap of the ears, from the physical stance of the elephant to the sound it creates through its trunk; the elephant is engaged in a continuous flow of communication. Experts tell us that those communication channels are not limited to the aural or the visual; elephants also communicate through the secretion of various chemicals that help communication over time and distance. These animals use these various and complex modes of communication as part and parcel of a rich social environment that is both fluid and constantly on the move. Perhaps unsurprisingly, in the social world of elephants, there is a great deal of altruism and collaboration. And in that rich social environment, the influence of the matriarch – the oldest, most experienced female – is paramount. She has an incredible social memory; a memory of friends and foes gathered over many years that enables her to support and nurture the herd.

Even before reaching the end of Chapter 1, we chose the elephant as a symbol for one of our central arguments. We did that because (ignoring the bear pit of political correctness) one of our clearest drivers to write this book had been the importance of so-called 'feminine qualities' for a networked world. These include the ability to perceive shades of grey, to build and nurture new and existing networks, to operate across boundaries, to value diversity, and amidst all that, the ability to empathize – to see the world through the eyes of those different from ourselves.

However, our journey over the last three years has been to see that "network brilliance" is not enough. Of course the right behaviors to build networks that yield the right sort of social capital are important, but what our observations and our interviews with real leaders solving real problems have taught us is the danger of what we have called "one circle insufficiency": an overly strong concentration on network behaviors to the detriment of other important leadership capabilities. More pointedly, those leadership conversations have stressed the importance of other aspects of leadership that we have subsumed under the headings of "strategic resilience" and "cognitive flexibility." There is no doubt that we achieve great results through others, but leaders need to have a clear sense of purpose in order to realize the advantage offered by the social capital they have at their disposal.

Our world has experienced a lot since 2006: India launched its first lunar probe, a clear sign of ever-growing financial power of Asian economies; Tony Blair handed the heavy mantle to his Chancellor of the Exchequer; the cost of oil per barrel soared sending the price of petrol at pumps across the world through the roof; and Barack Obama became the President of the United States of America. We have also witnessed the greatest economic meltdown since the Great Depression. Three years ago we went about our lives wrapped in what seemed to be the impregnable cocoon of modern capitalism, but between the Autumn of 2007 and the Spring of 2009, the world held its breath after realizing that the perceived invincibility of the global economy was yet another man-made illusion. As we write these words, the global economy has arrived at a position that is as precarious as it should have been predictable: and beneath it all is the poisonous accretion of the wrong sort of social capital.

One of the more poignant stories that illustrates how this mael-strom touched the lives of the unlikeliest of people is documented in David Faber's *And Then the Roof Caved In*, a pithy and comprehensible account of the financial collapse.[1] In his book, Faber, an award win-ning reporter for CNBC, spends an entire chapter highlighting the case of a small town in Norway and how the financial crisis had crippled its local infrastructure. Narvik is tiny: the total population is about 18,000. One of the town's more pressing fiscal challenges had been to swell its coffers despite an increasingly ageing demographic and the departure of its youth to fairer Norwegian cities such as Oslo. Amidst a range of investment strategies, Narvik's financial advisors proposed that the town invest in what seemed to be a wonderful investment instrument: the collateralized debt obligation (CDO).

The CDO is a security that is created by an investment bank when it buys thousands of home loans and then uses that security to finance the purchase. Investors who purchase a CDO make their money from the interest paid on those home loans. The quality of the CDO is decided by a credit rating which is in turn decided by the degree of risk of pos-sible non-payment of those home loans. The CDO itself is composed of a cocktail of home loans that vary in terms of financial risk. The CDOs that were perceived to have the least amount of risk attached to them were given an AAA credit rating. Narvik's advisors considered the secu-rities, along with many, many people around the world, to be a safe and sensible investment strategy for the town's public purse.

As we all know, the problem with this seemingly nifty, low risk investment is that many of the CDOs should never have received an AAA rating: many of the underlying mortgages were high risk, "sub-prime" loans and constituted a highly risky venture. Nevertheless, the credit rating agencies continued to give these instruments the coveted AAA rating. When payments on those sub-prime mortgages started to fail to appear, the real value of the CDOs became apparent and the whole global market began to unravel. For a small town like Narvik, the effect was catastrophic. The unexpected depletion of civic funds resulted in fewer teachers and larger classroom sizes; reduced personnel in nursing homes and the closure of Narvik's most popular tourist attraction – a museum dedicated to a famous World War II battle.

The frenzied purchase of CDOs by all sorts of investors around the world and the subsequent light-speed disintegration of this same market has exposed the unstable financial positions of small towns, whole countries and the sort of corporate giants that people thought would always be part of the commercial landscape. The crisis has touched everyone from respectable investment banks such as Lehman Brothers to giant manufacturers such as General Motors. If organizations are not impacted directly by risky investment strategies, then the collapse in confidence in the global economy and the drought of demand that has followed resulted in the destruction of the fragile, debt-laden companies who were living a daily existence invisibly on the edge.

As the saying goes, hindsight is always 20:20. Yet it is not the power of retrospect that should have enabled us to recognize the writing on the walls of financial institutions, governments, regulatory authorities, investment houses and the like; there was enough hard research and clear thinking in existence that should have enabled us to avoid the almost apocalyptic collapse of the global financial infrastructure. And some of it dates back as far as WW II. In 1942, the erudite and free-thinking economist Joseph Schumpeter published *Capitalism, Socialism & Democracy*, a book that cut across the traditional boundaries of many intellectual disciplines – economic, sociology, philosophy, history to name just a few.[2] It is a book that has important messages about the nature of capitalism and in which Schumpeter discusses his views about an intrinsic and unavoidable aspect of capitalism: what he memorably called "creative destruction."

Schumpeter lived a peripatetic life. He was born in 1883 in the now Czech Republic, grew up in Austria and before writing this book had lived in eleven cities and several countries. His interests led him to study psychology, history, economics and sociology. His professional life was as varied as his interests: he spent time in academia at some of the best universities in the world; as the secretary of state for Finance in Austria; and as the leader of an Austrian bank. The diverse nature of his friendships, his interests and professional pursuits across an international network enabled Schumpeter to develop a perspective on economics that did not fall into a particular school of thought, but which remained independent and unique. His professional experience and academic expertise led Schumpeter to develop a dynamic view of capitalism. In short, Schumpeter led a life of bridging.

For him, capitalism was an evolutionary process. He saw capitalism as both constantly changing and taking place within an environment that included social factors that are perilous and impossible to ignore. Our view is that a core social factor that played such a huge role in the recent economic explosion was the build up and dominance of the "wrong form" of social capital. Wherever we look at this "domino disaster," we see that the institutions, and ultimately the individuals who ran those institutions, had existed in a shared view of the world that was no different to the disastrous groupthink of the Kennedy cabinet that sanctioned the invasion of the Bay of Pigs. In Schumpeter's endless studies of economic systems, businesses and sociology, he recognized not only that the system of capitalism implied constant change, but also that the agents of that system, that is, we, have a deep-seated resistance to change – particularly when we are on to what seems like a good thing. In our recent financial world, there was no room for diversity of opinion or viewpoint or philosophy. No one wanted to disagree when everyone seemed to be winning. At the end of another recent book that charts the hubris of that socio-economic climate, *The House of Cards* by William Cohan, the author interviews a very senior member of that community who concludes, "We all fucked up. Government. Ratings agencies. Wall street. Commercial investors. Regulators. Everybody."[3]

If ever there has been a time for leaders to learn the lessons of the past and to demonstrate the skills of network leadership; to operate outside the claustrophobic barriers of their own insular worlds, to introduce diversity of people and perspective, to find solutions that serve not just short-term goals but long-term values, to build the absolutely right balance of social capital where bridging and bonding, consensus and debate can co-exist, then surely that time has to be now.

There is another way in which the context has shaped our conclusions and reinforced our arguments. If we had concluded this book eighteen months ago, the themes of Chapter 2 might have seemed premature or even a little naïve. When we wrote about the importance of networked, collaborative structures for organizations two years ago, off the page and out in the world, there seemed to be the opposite trend where "big is best." Organizations continued to acquire and merge in the desire to drive growth. Cash flow by itself was not enough; debt was the real fuel of perceived success. The recent demise of organizations that swallowed too much debt, that had grown too large to innovate and adapt effectively, returns us to the importance of the flatter collaborative enterprises. A deftly written article that appears in the June 2009 edition of *Wired* magazine looks closely at the car industry in the USA. The author, Chris Anderson, points out that the monolithic car manufacturers of Detroit have been notoriously resistant to innovation. In the world post meltdown, investment capital that is available to support organizations has gone in search of smaller companies where creativity has not been strangled. These organizations are flat, collaborative and connected, both to new ideas and also to a variety of people that enable them to move at real speed in pursuit of their goals. In the current climate we see the network organization, or more precisely the "collaborative enterprise," as the most effective form of organization to enable innovation, growth and prosperity in these uncertain times.

***

Are network leaders who value diversity, who are comfortable with complexity, who blur the boundaries of culture, geography and class and who can tell great stories too much to ask for? On January 21, 2009, the United States of America inaugurated their forty-fourth President. President Barack Hussein Obama was born to a white American mother and a black Kenyan father; he was brought up as a Christian in Hawaii and with a Muslim family in Kenya; he lived in the United States and Indonesia; became a lawyer who moved on to be the first non-white editor of the Harvard Law Review; is reported to admire Lincoln's predilection for putting people of opposing views into his cabinet; and has shown his considerable ability for oration and storytelling in his speeches, his interviews and in the books he has written. President Obama has already demonstrated all the qualities of what we have called network leadership in everything he has tackled to-date; of course, it remains to be seen whether these abilities translate effectively onto the world stage. Is President Obama just a new and bright shining moon hanging low over the horizon of the hopes and dreams of millions of people? We will let him have the last words. In his 2009 speech to Muslim leaders, he demonstrated all the sensibilities of a man who places enormous emphasis on seeing and understanding a shared context and who recognizes the irrefutable importance of interconnections of countries, governments and people around the world:

> For we have learned from recent experience that when a financial system weakens in one country, prosperity is hurt everywhere. When a new 'flu infects one human being, all are at risk. When one nation pursues a nuclear weapon, the risk of nuclear attack rises for all nations. When violent extremists operate in one stretch of mountains, people are endangered across an ocean. And when innocents in Darfur and Bosnia are slaughtered, then it is a strain on our collective conscience. That is the responsibility we have to one another as human beings.
>
> This is a difficult responsibility to embrace. For human history has often been a record of nations and tribes subjugating one another to serve their own interests. Yet in this new age, such attitudes are self-defeating. Given our interdependence, any world order that elevates one nation or group of people over another, will inevitably fail. So whatever we think of the past, we must not be prisoners of it. Our problems must be dealt with through partnership; progress must be shared.
>
> (Barack Obama, June 2009)[4]

MIRRORS IN THE BRAIN

We began our argument in Chapter 1 with the illusions and insights of an early twentieth-century psychologist; we conclude our book with the imaginative thoughts of a twenty-first-century equivalent in order to speculate about the origins of the leadership illusion. V. S. Ramachandran is an Indian-born neurologist, Director of the Centre for Brain and Cognition at the University of California, and is a modern master of illusions. Born of parents with a scientific bent, originally

Ramachandran enrolled at the medical school of the University of Madras in order to become a doctor. During his second year, inspired by conversations with his uncle – a professor of optics at the University of Sydney – the young Ramachandran turned his creative and enquiring mind to design an experiment about visual perception that went on to be published in the prestigious journal *Nature* before he had even graduated. Once he had graduated, Ramachandran moved on to do a PhD in visual perception at the University of Cambridge. There, he met someone who became a long-term collaborator, Professor Richard Gregory, a fellow fanatic for the visual system from Bristol University, and together over the next decade they wrote a number of papers in the field.

Eventually, Ramachandran moved out of visual perception and concentrated his attention on researching and investigating damage to the brain, both to understand what this might tell us about brain functionality but also to investigate whether the brain possessed inherent plasticity or, as many people believed, retained a fixed and modular purpose throughout a lifetime. One piece of research in this arena that has gained him an international reputation both as an innovative thinker and a rigorous scientific detective is his work with patients who suffered from the phantom limb phenomenon, that is, the continuing feeling of pain in a limb that has been amputated. Ramachandran's simple but insightful experiments revealed that the cause of the phantom limb phenomenon could be traced to changes in brain functionality. To understand this discovery, first we need to know that there are neuronal "maps" of our own body in the brain. When we move our arm, for example, the neurons in the body map that are related to this arm will fire. Of course, if someone has an arm amputated, those corresponding neurons should remain forever quiet. Ramachandran discovered that, in fact, what happens is that neurons in nearby areas of the brain, and which are responsible for processing stimuli from the face, actually "invade" the area responsible for the amputated arm. This means that stimulating areas of the face then causes neurons to fire in the arm area of the brain, creating illusory sensations in a phantom limb. These insights tell us something not only about brain plasticity, but also provide hints at possible treatments for phantom limbs.

In a recent profile of the man and his work in the *New Yorker* magazine, Ramachandran discussed one of his more recent pursuits in neural investigation.[5] Mirror neurons are brain cells that were originally discovered in the frontal lobes of monkeys. These neurons fire both when a monkey is reaching for an object, but also when observing another monkey performing the same action. Ramachandran and his colleagues used electroencephalogram (EEG) techniques successfully to find evidence of the same neurons in human beings. During his interview in the *New Yorker*, Ramachandran points out the increasing evidence that mirror neurons play a role in human empathy; they seem to allow us to construct a view of the world as seen through the eyes of other people. Mirror neurons, according to the argument, enable us to build that alternative perspective in our mind's eye.

Ramachandran, like any student of the brain, is drawn to a fundamental question: how does consciousness occur? He has speculated that those same mirror neurons may make their own contribution to the phenomenon of consciousness by allowing us to build a mental model of our own internal world, thereby enabling reflection on our own thoughts and emotions. Ramachandran's thoughts are tentative, but they suggest an interesting irony for the leadership illusion.

Ramachandran's speculative hypothesis seems to be that mirror neurons have evolved from cells that originally enabled us to model the internal world of others and so empathize with people. Those cells then evolved so that we could create a model of our own inner world, so contributing to reflexive thought and ultimately consciousness. That conscious world, a place in our minds where we can hear our thoughts and consider our feelings, also creates a sense of individual personal identity that seems distinct and separate from the world, an independent entity divorced from our context and other human beings. Indeed, mirror neurons that model the internal world of other people may also function to create that same illusory view of other people: independent entities isolated from their broader context and the invisible connections that bind people together.

The extent to which these speculations hold any truth is obviously a moot point: in terms of a theory of consciousness, as of 2009, nobody has it and possibly nobody is close. What is true is that as human beings we do struggle hard to see our connectedness to the world around us and to each other. Whether leader or follower, we need to consciously recognize we are all no more and no less than the sum of our relationships with others, our total social capital. Some of that social capital will be derived from bonding to people close to us; other elements will be drawn by bridging to people we don't yet know. Accepting this simple fact may prove to be the hardest leadership challenge of all.

Notes

INTRODUCTION: MAKING CONNECTIONS AND SHIFTING PERSPECTIVES

1. Will Hutton, *The State We're In* (Vintage; new edition, 1996).
2. Confucius, *The Analects* (Penguin Classics, 2003).
3. Sun Tzu, *The Art of War* (Filiquarian Publishing, 2006).
4. Malcolm Gladwell, *The Tipping Point* (Abacus New edition, 2002).
5. Malcolm Gladwell, *Blink* (Penguin, 2006).
6. Malcolm Gladwell, *Outliers: The Story of Success* (Allen Lane, 2008).

1 THE LEADERSHIP ILLUSION

1. Edgar Rubin, "Figure-Ground Perception," in *Readings in Perception*. Translated from German by M. Wertheimer (Van Nostrand, 1958) (Original work published in 1915).
2. David Remnick (ed.), *The New Gilded Age: The New Yorker Looks at the Culture of Affluence* (Modern Library, expanded edition, 2001).
3. Malcolm Gladwell, *Outliers: The Story of Success* (Allen Lane, 2009).
4. Alex Gibney, *Enron: The Smartest Guys in the Room* (Lions Gate Home Ent. UK Ltd, 2005).
5. Warren Bennis, *On Becoming a Leader* (Basic Books, revised edition, 2009).
6. Rudolph Giuliani, *Leadership* (Sphere, new edition, 2003).
7. Scientific American Mind (Scientific American Inc., April 2006).
8. Howard Gardner, *Leading Minds: An Anatomy of Leadership* (HarperCollins Publishers Ltd, new edition, 1997).
9. Beverly Alimo Metcalfe, *Leadership Development in British Organisations* (Careers Research Forum, 2000).
10. Steven J. Rubenzer and Thomas R. Faschingbauer, *Personality, Character and Leadership in the White House* (Potomac Books Inc, new edition, 2005).
11. Fidel Castro, *My Life*, translated by Andrew Hurley (Penguin, 2008).
12. Jones Edward, E. & Victor Harris, A., "The Attribution of Attitudes," *Journal of Experimental Social Psychology*, 3 (1967): 1–24.

13. Lee Ross, "The Intuitive Psychologist and His Shortcomings: Distortions in the Attribution Process," in L. Berkowitz (ed.), *Advances in Experimental Social Psychology*, vol. 10, (Academic Press, 1977), pp. 173–220.
14. Thomas L. Friedman, *The World is Flat: The Globalized World in the Twenty-first Century* (Penguin, 2nd revised edition, 2007).
15. Jeffrey S. Young and William L. Simon, *iCon Steve Jobs: The Greatest Second Act in the History of Business* (John Wiley & Sons, 2005).
16. For a biography of Max Weber, see Joachim Radkau, *Max Weber: A Biography* (Polity Press, 2009).
17. Maximillan Weber, "The Nature of Charismatic Authority and its Routinization," *Theory of Social and Economic Organization*, A. R. Anderson and Talcott Parsons (translators) (Macmillan, USA, 1964).
18. For a link to this experiment, see www.channel4.com/science/microsites/F/famelab/experiment/experiment.html
19. Malcolm Gladwell, *The Tipping Point: How Little Things Can Make a Big Difference* (Abacus, new edition, 2002).
20. Paul Ekman and Wallace V. Friesen, *Unmasking the Face: A Guide to Recognizing Emotions from Facial Expressions* (Malor Books, 2003).
21. For an account of Simmel's work see Kurt H. Wolff, *The Sociology Of George Simmel* (The Free Press, 1950).
22. Boas Shamir, Rajnandini Pillai, Michelle C. Bligh and Mary Uhl-Bien (eds.), *Follower-centered Perspectives on Leadership: A Tribute to the Memory of James R. Meindl*, in Leadership Horizons (Information Age Publishing, 2007).
23. Albert Einstein, *Relativity* (Routledge, 2nd edition, 2001).

2   OUR CONNECTED WORLD

1. Bill Gates and Collins Hemingway, *Business at the Speed of Thought: Succeeding in the Digital Economy* (Penguin, new edition, 2000).
2. John Urry, *Global Complexity* (Polity Press, 2002).
3. www.**secondlife**.com
4. Manuel Castells, *The Rise of the Network Society: Economy, Society and Culture* (Wiley Blackwell, 2nd edition, 2000).
5. Will Hutton, *The World We're In* (Little Brown, 2002).
6. See Eric Von Hippel's homepage at http://web.mit.edu/evhippel/www/
7. Kjell Nordstrom and Jonas Ridderstrale, *Funky Business* (ft. com, 1999).
8. Jeffrey Pfeffer and Robert Sutton, *The Knowing-Doing Gap: How Smart Companies Turn Knowledge into Action* (Harvard Business School Press, 1999).
9. John Hagel III and John Seely Brown, *The Only Sustainable Edge: Why Business Strategy Depends on Productive Friction and Dynamic Sepcialization* (Harvard Business School Press, 2005).
10. See for example: Mark A. Huselid and Brian E Becker, *The HR Scorecard: Linking People, Strategy, and Performance* (Harvard Business School Press, 2001).

11. See, for example, Mark Thompson, "Added Value through High Performance Workplaces," in John Storey, (ed.) *Adding Value through Information and Consultation*, (Palgrave Macmillan, 2005).
12. The Work Foundation, *Cracking the Performance Code: How Firms Succeed* (The Work Foundation, 2005).
13. John Guare, *Six Degrees of Separation* (Vintage Books, 1990).
14. Although much quoted in the literature, Karinthy's short stories are no longer in print. However, for more information about Karinthy and his story 'Chains' see, Albert-Laszlo Barabasi, *Linked: The New Science of Networks* (Perseus Books, 2003).
15. Stanley Milgram, *Obedience to Authority* (HarperCollins, 1974).
16. For a contemporary commentary see, Thomas Blass (ed.), *Obedience to Authority: Current Perspectives on the Milgram Paradigm* (Psychology Press, 2000).
17. Jeffrey Travers and Stanley Milgram, "An Experimental Study of the Small World Problem," *Sociometry*, vol. 32, no. 4 (1969): 425–443.
18. Mark Granovetter, *Getting a Job: Study of Contacts and Careers* (Harvard University Press, 1974).
19. François-René de Chateaubriand, *The Memoirs of Chateaubriand* (Penguin, 1965).
20. See, for example, Martin Heidegger, *Being and Time* (Wiley-Blackwell, 1978).
21. Richard Reeves, *Happy Mondays: Putting the Pleasure Back into Work* (Momentum, 2001).
22. John Stuart Mill, *On Liberty* (Longman, new edition, 2007).

3   THE RIGHT SORT OF SOCIAL CAPITAL

1. For more on the *Times* 100 best companies follow this link: http://business.timesonline.co.uk/tol/business/career_and_jobs/best_100_companies/
2. The Work Foundation, *Cracking the Performance Code: How Firms Succeed* (The Work Foundation, 2005).
3. Robert D. Putnam, *Bowling Alone: The Collapse and Revival of American Community* (Simon & Schuster, 2000).
4. See, for example, D. Swartz, *Culture and Power: Sociology of Pierre Bourdieu* (Chicago University Press, 1998).
5. James Coleman, "Social Capital in the Creation of Human Capital," *American Journal of Sociology*, Supplement, 94 (1988): S95–S120.
6. See, for example, Anatol Rapoport and Albert M. Chammah, *Prisoner's Dilemma* (University of Michigan Press, 1965).
7. *The Dark Knight* (Warner Bros., 2008).
8. Ronald S. Burt, *Brokerage and Closure: An Introduction to Social Capital* (Oxford University Press, 2007).

9. James C. Collins and Jerry I. Porras, *Built to Last: Successful Habits of Visionary Companies* (Random House Business Books, new edition, 2005).

10. Martin Kilduff and Wenpin Tsai, *Social Networks and Organizations* (Sage Publications Ltd, 2003).

11. Neville Stanton (ed.), *Human Factors in Nuclear Safety*, (Taylor and Francis, 1996).

12. Francis Fukuyama, *Trust: The Social Virtues and the Creation of Prosperity* (The Free Press, 1996).

13. Philip G. Zimbardo, *The Lucifer Effect: How Good People Turn Evil* (Rider & Co, 2008).

14. David Halpern, *Social Capital* (Polity Press, new edition, 2004).

4   MAKING THE INVISIBLE VISIBLE

1. Michael Frayn, *The Human Touch. Our Part in the Creation of a Universe* (Faber and Faber, 2007).

2. Elton Mayo, *Hawthorne and the Western Electric Company: The Social Problems of an Industrial Civilisation* (Routledge, 1949).

3. Bruce Kapferer, *Strategy and Transaction in an African Factory: African Workers and Indian Management in a Zambian Town* (Manchester University Press, 1972).

4. Ian Parker, *Granta 1971*, Shrinks www.granta.com/Magazine/71

5. To visit the Oracle of Elvis follow this link: http://www.cs.virginia.edu/oracle/elvis.html

6. Malcolm Gladwell, "In the Air: Who Says Big Ideas Are Rare?" *New Yorker*, May 12, 2008.

7. Albert-Laszlo Barabasi and Jennifer Frangos, *Linked: The New Science of Networks* (Perseus Books, 2003).

8. Duncan J. Watts, *Six Degrees: The New Science of Networks* (New Vintage, 2004).

9. See "The Social Graph of a Famous Mathematician," www.orgnet.com/Eredos.html

10. Kurt Lewin, *Resolving Social Conflicts: Field Theory in Social Science* (American Psychological Association, reprinted edition, 1997).

11. Isabel Briggs Myers, *Gifts Differing: Understanding Personality Type* (Davies-Black Publishing, reprint edition, 1995).

12. Ronald S. Burt, "Personality Correlates of Structural Holes," in Roderick M. Kramer and Margaret A. Neale (eds.), *Power and Influence in Organizations* (Thousand Oaks: Sage Publications, 1998), pp. 221–50.

13. Beverly Alimo–Metcalfe, *Leadership Development in British Organisations* (Careers Research Forum, 2000).

5 THREE CIRCLES OF NETWORK LEADERSHIP

1. Richard Feynman, "Epilogue," in Tony Hey and Patrick Walters, *The New Quantum Universe* (Cambridge University Press, 2nd edition, 2003).
2. Bryan Sykes, *Adam's Curse: A Future without Men* (Corgi Books, new edition, 2004).
3. Helen Fisher, "The Natural Leadership Talents of Women," in Lin Coughlin, Ellen Wingard and Keith Hollihan (eds.), *Enlightened Power: How Women Are Transforming the Practice of Leadership* (Jossey Bass, 2005).
4. Simon Baron-Cohen, *The Essential Difference* (Penguin, new edition, 2004).
5. To see their autism test go to www.autismresearchcentre.com
6. R. J. Spiro, P. J. Feltovich, M. J. Jacobson and R. L. Coulson, "Cognitive Flexibility, Constructivism and Hypertext: Random Access Instruction for Advanced Knowledge Acquisition in Ill-structured Domains," in T. Duffy and D. Jonassen (eds.), *Constructivism and the Technology of Instruction* (Hillsdale, NJ: Erlbaum, 1992)
7. Roger L. Martin, *The Opposable Mind. How Successful Leaders Win through Integrative Thinking* (Harvard Business School Press, 2008).
8. Roger L. Martin, in *Business Week*, Special Report. Get Creative August 1, 2005.
9. The Work Foundation, *Cracking the Performance Code: How Firms Succeed* (The Work Foundation, 2005).
10. Daniel H. Pink, *A Whole New Mind. Why Right-brainers Will Rule the Future* (Marshall Cavendish Business, 2008).
11. Robert McKee, *Story* (Methuen Publishing Ltd, 1999).
12. For an example of Professor Edson's research see, Jennifer Edson Escalas, "Imagine Yourself in the Product: Mental Simulation, Narrative Transportation, and Persuasion," *Journal of Advertising*, vol. 33 (2004) : 37–48.
13. Henry Mintzberg, *The Rise and Fall of Strategic Planning* (Financial Times/ Prentice Hall, 2000).
14. Viktor E. Frankl, *Man's Search for Meaning: The Classic Tribute to Hope from the Holocaust* (Rider & Co, new edition, 2004).

6 THE LIGHT BULB ILLUSION

1. Aaron Sorkin, *The Farnsworth Invention* (2007).
2. Robert Friedel, Paul B. Israel and Bernard S. Finn. *Edison's Electric Light: Biography of an Invention* (Rutgers University Press, new edition, 1988).
3. To read more of Professor Hargadon's work visit http://andrewhargadon. com/or take a look at Andrew Hargadon, "Bridging and Building: Towards a Microsociology of Creativity," in Leigh Thompson (ed.), *Creativity and*

Innovation in Groups and Teams (Lawrence Erlbaum Associates, Inc. (forthcoming)).

4. Malcolm Gladwell, "The Televisionary. Big Business and the Myth of the Lone Inventor," *New Yorker*, May 27, 2002.
5. Mihaly Csikszentmihalyi, *Creativity* (HarperCollins, 1st Harper Perennial edn, 1996).
6. David Simon and Edward Burns *The Corner: A Year in the Life of an Inner-city Neighbourhood* (Canongate Books Ltd, 2009).
7. Don Tapscott and Anthony Williams, *Wikinomics* (Atlantic Books, 2008).
8. See McEwen, www.usnews.com. September 17, 2006.
9. See www.innocentive.com/
10. To view the McKinsey model visit www.mckinseyquarterly.com/Leadership_and_innovation_2089
11. See www.inthecompanyofactors.com/Andrew Upton.

7 LEADERSHIP DEVELOPMENT: OF FIRES AND FORGES

1. To read Steve Jobs' full commencement speech follow this link. http://news.stanford.edu/news/2005/june15/jobs-061505.html
2. J. Peter Killing, Thomas Malnight and Tracey Keys. *Must-Win Battles: Creating the Focus You Need to Achieve Your Key Business Goals* (Financial Times/Prentice Hall, 2005).
3. Andrew Kakabadse and Nada Kakabadse, *Leading the Board: The Six Disciplines of World Class Chairmen* (Palgrave Macmillan, 2007).
4. Visit www.performanceconsultants.co.uk to find out more about this coaching organization.
5. Ronald S Burt & D. Ronchi, "Teaching executives to see social capital: results from a field experiment," Social Science Research (2007).

8 ELEPHANTS, MOONS AND MIRRORS

1. David Faber, *And Then the Roof Caved In: How Wall Street Greed and Stupidity Brought Capitalism to Its Knees* (John Wiley & Sons, 2009).
2. Joseph Alois Schumpeter. *Capitalism, Socialism and Democracy* (Harper Perennial, 2008).
3. William D. Cohan, *House of Cards: How Wall Street's Gamblers Broke Capitalism: The Fall of Bear Stearns and the Collapse of the Global Market* (Allen Lane, 2009).
4. For a full transcript of Barack Omama's speech see: http://www.huffingtonpost.com/2009/06/04/obama-egypt-speech-video_n_211216.html
5. John Colapinto, profiles, "Brain Games," *The New Yorker*, May 11 (2009): 76.

INDEX

A

Abu Ghraib prison abuse   56
acquisitions and mergers   107, 162
action   133
Adam's Curse: A Future without Men
  (Sykes)   86
adaptation   xiii, 22
adaptive agency   60
advertisements   97
Affective Communication Test   16
Akzonobel Decorative Paints   101,
  138
Alimo-Metcalfe, Beverley   10, 81–2
Andersen, Hans Christian   3
Anderson, Chris   162
And Then the Roof Caved In
  (Faber)   159
anticipation   xiii, 22
Apple   130
art   116–17
attributes   8, 9–10, 14–17, 19
attributions   8, 10–13, 17–19
Audur Capital   89
Auschwitz   100–1

B

Baltimore drug gangs   120–1
banking   25
Barabasi, Albert-Laszlo   74, 75–6, 77
Baron-Cohen, Simon   87, 88, 90
Bate, Howard   60–3
Bennis, Warren   7–8
Blair, Tony   91, 159

Blink (Gladwell)   x
boards   134–5
  see also executive teams
Bohr, Niels   3
bonding capital   49, 63, 165
  exclusion   56
  executive teams   138, 141–2
  leadership styles   57, 58, 59
  see also social capital
Bourdieu, Pierre   44–5, 57
Bowling Alone (Putnam)   48
BP, *see* British Petroleum
brain processes   88, 164–5
Branson, Richard   14
Bridge, Liz   132–3
bridging capital   49, 62, 165
  executive teams   138, 141–2
  job hunting   53
  leadership styles   57, 58, 59
  see also social capital
Bristol   32, 33, 108–9
British Petroleum (BP)   103
brokerage   48, 49, 76, 81, 83
Brown, Gordon   25
Brown, John Seely   31
Built to Last (Collins & Porras)   51
Burns, Edward   120
Burt, Ron   48, 76, 78, 80,
  82, 150–1

C

calculus   74
Caltech (Californian Institute of
  Technology)   85

capitalism 160–1
Capitalism, Socialism & Democracy (Schumpeter) 160
Capone, Al 70
career paths 37–8
car industry 162
Cartwright, Jez 148–50
Cassani, Barbara 91
Castells, Manuel 24
Castro, Fidel 11–12, 54–5
CBI, *see* Confederation of British Industry
centralization 72, 76
Chait, Richard 7
Chapman, Clare 95–6, 98
character 9–10, 11
see also personality
charisma 13–19
attributes 14–17, 19
attributions 17–19
definition of 15
Chateaubriand, François-René de 36
Cheltenham Science Festival 102
Chernobyl disaster 55
Chicago 70
Chicago Booth School of Business 48, 80, 150–1
Churchill, Winston 13
civic engagement 47–8
Clinton, Bill 47
closure 48, 76, 81, 82, 83
coaching 136, 145–50
co-coaching 129
cognitive flexibility 91, 93–5, 109
Edison 113–14
feedback 145
innovation networks 125
cognitive theory of leadership 9–10
Cohan, William 161
Coleman, James 45, 46, 50
collaborative enterprises 120, 121, 122–3, 162

collateralized debt obligation (CDO) 159–60
Collins, James C. 51
common sense 2, 19–20
communication 33, 101, 141, 158
communities of practice 30
competencies 10
complexity xiii, 22, 39
concentration camps 100–1
Confederation of British Industry (CBI) xii–xiii
Confucius ix
consciousness 165
context xi, xiii–xiv, 7, 20
coaching 150
Enron scandal 6
Florentine Renaissance art 116–17
Fundamental Attribution Error 11, 12
gender differences 89
organizational 131–2, 152–6
social capital 42
strategic 134–5, 144, 145
wine 110
conversations 134–5
The Corner (Simon & Burns) 120
corruption 6, 25
Cranfield School of Management 132, 134
creative destruction 160
creativity 115, 116, 117, 162
Cronin, Bruce 65–6
Csikszentmihalyi, M. 116–17
cultural capital 44, 45
cultural differences
emotional expression 16–17
Fundamental Attribution Error 13

D

The Dark Knight (film) 45–6
Darwin, Charles 16
"deficit divas" 132

"degrees of separation"
  hypothesis   35, 36
  see also "small world
    phenomenon"
Denmark   3
development, *see* leadership
  development
diversity   49, 76
drugs   108–9, 120–1

E

e2v   96–7, 154–5
economic crisis   xii–xiii, 22, 25, 40,
  89, 159–62
economic risk   28
economy, global   24–6, 28, 159
Edison, Thomas   112–14, 116, 119
ego network maps   136–7
Einstein, Albert   2–3, 20, 79
Ekman, Paul   16
elephants   158
Eli Lilly   123
elitism   57
emotional capital   89
emotions
  contagious nature of   16
  display of   16–17
  leadership development   130–1
empathy   9, 89, 90
  as feminine quality   87–8, 158
  mirror neurons   165
  network excellence   93
  storytelling   97
employees
  involvement of   27, 31–5
  morale   131
  organizational context   131–2
  retention   151
  social capital   40–1
empowerment   82
energy, releasing   93, 101–3
Enron   4–5, 6
enterprise   119

entrepreneurial leaders   58, 63
entrepreneurial personality   80–1
entrepreneurship   53, 118, 119
environmental issues   28
Erdos, Paul   74–6, 77
Escalas, Jennifer Edson   97
The Essential Difference (Baron-
  Cohen)   90
Evans, Sir Christopher   91, 92, 93,
  117–20
evolutionary perspective   17
exclusion   56–7
executive education programs
  150–1
executive teams   134–5, 136–42
extroverts   77

F

Faber, David   159
facial expressions   15, 16, 17
FAE, *see* Fundamental Attribution
  Error
The Farnsworth Invention
  (Sorkin)   111, 125
Farnsworth, Philo   111–12, 114, 125
Faschingbauer, Thomas R.   10
feedback
  executive teams   137–8, 139
  motivation through   101
  360° feedback   81–2, 142–5
feminine qualities   87–8, 158
Feynman, Richard   85–6, 110
field theory   79
financial risk   28
Finn, Bernard   113
Fisher, Helen   87, 88, 90
flexibility
  cognitive   91, 93–5, 109, 113–14,
    125, 145
  network leadership   59–60
  outcome focus   99
Florence   116–17, 119
Frankl, Viktor   100–1

fraud 6
Frayn, Michael 65
Frederick, Ivan 56
Friedel, Robert 113
Friedman, Thomas 13, 15–16
Frito-Lay 55
Fukuyama, Francis 55
Fundamental Attribution Error
 (FAE) 11, 12–13
Funky Business (Nordstrom &
 Ridderstrale) 29

G

Game Theory 45
Gandhi, Mahatma 17
Gardner, Howard 9–10
Gates, Bill 7, 22, 57
gender differences 86–90
geographical mobility 23
George, Sir Eddie 91
Giuliani, Rudolf 8, 19
Gladwell, Malcolm x–xi, 6, 16,
 74, 114
Global Complexity (Urry) 23
global economy 24–6, 28, 159
globalization 30
global markets 27, 28–9
Goldcorp. 122
Gomes, Ieda 103–6
Gore, Al 96
Granovetter, Mark 36–7, 53
Greenwich Business School 65–6
Gregory, Richard 164
Groupthink 55, 161
Guare, John 35

H

Hagel, John III 31
Halpern, David 57
Happy Mondays (Reeves) 37
Hargadon, Andrew 114, 115–16,
 124, 136
Harris, Victor A. 11–12

Harvard Business School 5
Harvard Graduate School of
 Education 7
Hawthorne Studies 70–1
hierarchical structure 27, 28–9
The House of Cards (Cohan) 161
Hubble Telescope 83
The Human Touch (Frayn) 65
Huselid, Mark A. 31
Hutton, Will ix, 26, 43–4,
 54, 105

I

Iceland 89
iCon (Young & Simon) 14
IMD business school 134
incentives 71
India 159
industrial relations 72, 107
inequalities 23
informal relationships xiii, 71,
 155–6
informational advantage 27
information technology 23
Innocentive 122–3
innovation 27, 29, 118–20
 collaborative enterprises 121,
 122–3, 162
 large organizations 114
 leadership and 123–6
 "open source" 121–2
 P&G 94–5
 partnerships 115–16
 technical leaders 59
interactionist approach 69, 77–82
interdependence xiii, 24, 25–6, 27,
 39, 163
interdisciplinary approaches xiv, xvi
Internet xiii, 23–4
introverts 76–7
inventors 112, 114–15
Israel, Paul 113
Italian farmworkers xi

J

Jackson, Andrew 10
James, William 98
Jamieson, Paul 126
job hunting 53
Jobs, Steve 13–14, 130
Johnson, Lyndon B. 10
Jones, Edward E. 11–12

K

Kakabadse, Andrew 134–5, 137–8
Kapferer, Bruce 72–3
Kennedy, John F. 10, 13, 54–5, 161
Keys, Tracey 134
Kilduff, Martin 54
Killing, J. Peter 134
Kirkegaard, Søren 3
"Kitchener, Captain Jim" 128–9, 130, 131–2
knowledge 27, 29–30

L

Lafley, A. J. 94–5
language 68–9
Lay, Ken 5
leadership
    attribute-based approaches 9–10
    Castro 11
    charisma 13–14, 18
    commonsense view of 19–20
    conceptions of ix–x
    importance of context xiii–xiv, 20
    innovation and 123–6
    interdisciplinary analysis xiv
    mystique of 7–8
    purpose of 86
    social capital 57–60
    storytelling 96–7
    360° feedback 81–2, 142–5
    university 32–5
    see also network leadership

leadership development 127–56
    coaching 145–50
    emotional engagement 130–1
    evaluation of programs 132–3
    executive education 150–1
    irrelevancy of programs 129, 130
    organizational context 152–6
    pre-training assessment 133
    professional prejudices
        about 127–8
    social capital 135–42
    strategic context 134–5
    thoughts and behaviors 142–5
Leading Minds: An Anatomy of
    Leadership (Gardner) 10
learning 130, 133–4, 151, 152–3
Lee Kwan Yew 14
Leibniz, G. W. 74
Lerach, Bill 6
Lewin, Kurt 79
Li & Fung 30–1
Lidstone, Peter 98, 101–2, 103, 138–42
light bulb illusion 111, 113, 114–15, 117, 121, 126
Linux 122
logotherapy 100–1
loyalty 59
The Lucifer Effect: How Good People
    Turn Evil (Zimbardo) 56

M

Mac computers 130
Malnight, Thomas 134
managers 63, 81
Mandela, Nelson 17
Man's Search for Meaning
    (Frankl) 100–1
Martin, Roger 94–5
mathematical approach 69, 73–7
matrix organizational
    structure 154–5
Mayo, Elton 70–2

MBTI questionnaire 80
McEwen, Rob 122
McKee, Robert 96
McKinsey 5, 123, 124–5
McVeigh, Timothy 55
meetings 139, 140–1
Menlo Park 114
mergers and acquisitions 107, 162
Merlin Biosciences 92, 117–18, 119
Milgram, Stanley 35–7, 73
Mill, John Stuart 37
Milne, Stewart 100, 101
"mind reading" 9
Mintzberg, Henry 99
mirror neurons 164–5
morale 131
motivation 101, 150, 151
Mott MacDonald 60–3

N

Narvik 159–60
National Health Service (NHS) 95–6
Nazi concentration camps 100–1
Negroponte, Nicholas 23
Network Architects 106–9
Network Builders 105–6
network excellence 91, 93, 103–9
    Edison 114
    innovation networks 125
network leadership xiv, xv, 34–5,
    59–60, 90–109
    case study 60–3
    cognitive flexibility 93–5
    executive teams 138
    feedback 144–5
    global 26
    informal social structures 155–6
    innovation networks 125
    learning 133–4
    network excellence 103–9
    Obama 162–3
    realistic optimism 99–101
    releasing energy 101–3

storytelling 96–7
strategic resilience 97–9
see also leadership
networks xiv, xv, xvi, 20–1, 35–9,
    65–84
    drug gangs 121
    ego network maps 136–7
    global 23, 24, 26
    innovation 29, 124, 125
    interactionist approach 69,
        77–82
    language gaps 68–9
    mapping 66–8, 136–7, 145
    mathematical approach 69,
        73–7
    McKinsey 124–5
    organizational 26–8
    social capital 42, 48, 49, 54
    sociological approach 69, 70–3
    see also relationships; social capital
Network Sustainers 103–5
neurons 164–5
Newton, Isaac 74
New York Times 112–13
NHS, see National Health Service
Nigeria 128
Nixon, Richard 10
nurturing leaders 59

O

Obama, Barack 159, 162–3
obedience experiments
    (Milgram) 35–6
One Laptop per Child
    Association 23
"open source" 121–2
The Opposable Mind (Martin) 94–5
optimism 93, 98, 99–101, 132
The Oracle of Elvis 73–4
organizational context 131–2,
    152–6
organizational structure 27, 28–9,
    89, 154–5, 156

outcomes   93, 97–9, 135
Outliers: The Story of Success
   (Gladwell)   x, xi

P

P&G, *see* Proctor & Gamble
Parker, Ian   73
people skills   90
Pepsi   55
perception   1–2, 3–4, 157, 164
perfectionism   98
performance
   coaching impact on   149, 150
   collaboration between
      organizations   53
   entrepreneurial networks   81
   executive education
      programs   151
   high-performance
      organizations   27, 31–5,
      40–1, 95
   knowledge about   30
   team   124
personality   9, 78
   charisma   15
   "entrepreneurial"   80–1
   trait-based approach   79–80
*Personality, Character and Leadership
   in the White House* (Rubenzer &
   Faschingbauer), 10
Peters, Tom   5
Pfeffer, Jeffrey   30
phantom limb phenomenon   164
Phillips, Sam   115–16
physics   2–3, 20, 79
   see also science
Pink, Dan   96
Plutarch   127
political risk   28
Porras, Jerry I.   51
presidents   10
Presley, Elvis   73–4, 77, 115–16
priorities   134

Prisoner's Dilemma   45–6
prison experiment (Zimbardo)   56
Proctor & Gamble (P&G)   94–5
Prohibition Era   70
psychology   2, 79, 84
   Fundamental Attribution
      Error   11, 12–13
   personality   9, 78
   social comparison theory   19
public sector   119
"pull" economy   28, 30–1
"push" economy   27–8
Putnam, Robert D.   42, 47–8, 50,
   54, 55

R

R&D, *see* research & development
Ramachandran, V. S.   163–5
random graphs   75–6, 77
rational choice theory   46
Raytheon   150–1
realistic optimism   98, 99–101
reciprocity   101–2, 103
Reeves, Richard   37
reflection   133
relationships   32, 41, 61–3, 76–7
   bridging and bonding   49
   ego network maps   136–7
   executive teams   135, 136–7,
      138–9, 140
   human behavior   79
   informal   xiii, 71, 155–6
   innovation   120
   Network Sustainers   103, 104–5
   nurturing leaders   59
   sociological approach   69
   see also networks; social capital
Remnick, David   6
Renaissance   116–17
Renyi, Albert   75–6, 77
research & development
   (R&D)   118, 121
resistance to change   71, 161

return on investment (ROI)   132, 133
The Rise and Fall of Strategic Planning
   (Mintzberg)   99
risk   27, 28–9, 118, 159–60
ROI, *see* return on investment
Roosevelt, Franklin Delano   10
Roosevelt, Theodore   10
Ross, Lee   12
Rowling, J. K.   22
Rubenzer, Steven J.   10
Rubin, Edgar   3–4

S

sacrifice   46–7
Salter, Chuck   5
sanctions   52
Sarnoff, David   112
Schumpeter. Joseph   160–1
science   87, 102, 107–8
   see also physics
Scraton, Peter   71–2, 96–7, 107,
   154–5
Second Life   24
Shamir, Boas   18
Simmel, Georg   17–18
Simon, David   120
Simon, William L.   14
simultaneous discovery,
   phenomenon of   74
Singapore   14
Six Degrees of Separation (Guare)   35
Six Degrees (Watts)   79
Skilling, Jeff   4–7, 12, 25
"small world phenomenon"   36,
   73–4, 75, 77
Smith, Adam   89
Snook, Hans   91–2
social capital   40–64, 69, 82–3,
   158–9, 165
   benefits of   50–4
   Bourdieu   44–5
   dark side of   54–7
   definitions of   41–4, 50

executive education
   programs   151
feedback   144, 145
Florentine Renaissance art   116–17
impact on performance   32
implications for leadership   57–60
leadership development   135–42
McKinsey   124–5
Network Architects   106
network excellence   93
Prisoner's Dilemma   45–6
wrong form of   40, 159, 161
see also networks; relationships
Social Capital (Halpern)   57
social comparison theory   19
social context, *see* context
social distance   18
social intelligence   90, 104
social networking sites   xiii
social rules   71
sociological approach   69, 70–3
Sorkin, Aaron   111, 112
Spiro, R. J.   94
"step thinking"   87
storytelling   96–7
St Pauls, Bristol   108
strategic alliances   52–3
strategic context   134–5, 144, 145
strategic planning   99
strategic resilience   91, 93,
   97–9, 109
   Edison   114
   feedback   145
   innovation networks   125
   "strength optimists"   132
strikes   72
Sun Tzu   ix
supply chain networks   27, 30–1
support   54, 104
Sutton, Robert   30
Sykes, Brian   86
Sykes, Kathy   87, 102–3, 107–9
"systematizing"   87, 88, 90

T

Tapscott, Don 121–2
team development 137–8
team performance 124
  see also executive teams
technical leaders 58–9
"technology brokers" 114, 119
television 111, 112
theater 125–6
Thomas, Eric 32–5, 47
Thompson, Mark 31
360° feedback 81–2, 142–5
The Tipping Point (Gladwell) x, 16
Tomasdottir, Halla 89
Top 100 organizations 40
Toronto School of Business 94
training
  empathy 9
  evaluation of 132–3
  workshops 152–3
  see also leadership development
traits 79–80
transformational leadership 10
trust 25, 63, 101–2
  executive teams 136, 139, 140
  innovative partnerships 116
  McKinsey 125
  nurturing leaders 59
  organizational context 155
  social capital 50
Tsai, Wenpin 54

U

Uganda 23
university leadership 32–5
Upton, Andrew 125
Urry, John 23

V

values 96
Vanderbilt School of
  Management 97

virtual worlds 24
volunteers 102
Von Hippel, Eric 29

W

Watts, Duncan J. 74, 75–6, 77, 79
Weber, Max 14–15
"web thinking" 87, 89
Western Electric Company
  (WEC) 70–1
The West Wing (TV show) 111
Wharton Business School 123
Wheelwright, Sally 88
Whole New Mind (Pink) 96
Wikinomics (Tapscott &
  Williams) 121–2
Williams, Anthony 121–2
wine 85, 86, 110
The Wire (TV show) 120
Wiseman, Richard 15
WLB, *see* work life balance
women 59, 86–90
  see also feminine qualities
work and career paths 37–8
The Work Foundation 31–2, 40, 95
work life balance (WLB) 37–8
workshops 152–3
The World is Flat (Friedman) 13

Y

Young, Jeffrey S. 14

Z

Zambia 72
Zimbardo, Phillip 56
Zworykin, Vladimir 112